AF614049

Afterlife Reflections ~ Pieces of Soul

by John E. Peterson, CHt

A Soul's Journey;
experiencing lessons through
multiple life-times

Afterlife Reflections ~ Pieces of Soul
A Soul's Journey; experiencing lessons through multiple life-times

Cover design: Unknown Photo; Modified John Peterson

ISBN #: 978-1-105-05614-7

Contents

Afterlife Reflections: Pieces of Soul

by John Peterson

This book is from my Soul.

Introduction

"Anyone can achieve their fullest potential. Who we are might be pre-determined but the path we follow is always of our own choosing. We should never allow our fears, or the expectations of others to set the frontiers of our destiny. Your destiny can't be changed, but it can be challenged. Every man is born as many men and dies as a single man." ~ anonymous

I have found many times in this lifetime that a 'déjà vu' experience surprises me when I'm not looking. It makes me stop and think for a moment of the meaning, the actions required at the moment, what lead this moment to actually present itself just then. Is it a synchronicity of our present life that allows these moments to emerge? In this lifetime we are guided into different situations that have been determined to be our interpreted lessons.

Many books have been written regarding our past lives, and the bridge to the afterlife and are focused on our personal experiences with the loss of our loved one. While we all physically die eventually, we need to keep in mind the ‘essence’ of the Soul. When we die it is said that the physical body losses weight. Is this the essence of the Soul?

It has been measured at 21 grams. Even a movie has been produced about the 21 grams. I suppose that is the concentrated weight of our lifetimes! It’s just a theory.

On this world, in the here and now, most think of the Soul as a ‘thing’. For me, looking out into a crowd, the Soul looks like a Lava lamp, about 14” tall and filled with a shimmering, fluid, silver and gold bright light. Everyone looks the same to me. I compare the brightness of the light with that of the eye test the eye doctor shines into your eyes. Mostly the brightness only varies with faith or conviction. Having a strong awareness and belief systems helps to keep the light bright. When the human side of us or ego is in control, the light diminishes and you stand alone.

I have found that people who have chosen to investigate their spiritual path and intuition feeds the light. We what we seek are the people who seek each other’s light, the Soul in others. We are then drawn collectively with the inner knowing of who people are. The connection we have to the universe around us does also vary in size. That connection can be seen as thin as a thread or as broad as ones shoulders. Faith and awareness determine this connection. When I look out into a crowd, the Souls all look the same. Why not, we are all from the same source.

Sometimes the idea of a Soul is difficult to comprehend. At death, it is said that the Soul leaves the body. People have seen their loved ones standing next to them. When they have left their message, they continue their journey to enter the 'light'. The light is the 'essence' of the Soul I speak here about. The essence contains this memory and the memories of all of its experiences. Albert Einstein has said, 'Physics teaches us that energy cannot be destroyed'.

So what is the true essence of your Soul? While Mediums can connect with the 'personality of the Soul' or memory of our lost family member or friend of their last lifetime, the Soul remains to be the essence of itself. The lost one's connection is but a memory to the Soul. So imagine the essences of all the Souls, people around you. The essence or memory stays with us throughout our life time. When we ourselves cross, that memory of who we knew returns to its own Soul's essence. One that holds the memory of their last lifetime is completed, the essence or energy of the Soul disperses and returns to its origin. This is typically 60 to 80 human years.

As a Hypnotherapist, I often return people to examine their past lives. Clues to 'who we were' tend to be parts of experiences we live and relive in this lifetime. When clients are asked to return to 'their first existence' the Soul travels to the memory of its creation point. The point of its birth or origin. When asked to describe this place, all of them have expressed a similar theme, a similar existence. I'll not share that place with you here. It is personal and needs to be experienced on your own, to visit your own point of creation.

The events or patterns we choose in each lifetime to experience are designed to guide us. In this lifetime, for us as individuals, we are awakening to our own intuition, remembering the feelings, emotions and learning of the past lives that we contain. Learning these things about ourselves is the key to our own growth as spiritual beings.

The following story represents several lifetimes of a particular Souls' journey. It represents the experiences toward awareness in each life-time. Our true awakening to our gifts. Each lifetime showing us an emotion, a pattern or a moment of awareness. The important part of these moments are the goals or lessons being presented. The time of our life's departure from the physical and the return to the essence of Soul allows us to see and learn what growth has been presented in each lifetime.

‘Afterlife Reflections: Pieces of Soul’

The Soul is a collection of a few experiences that the Soul has had since its’ origin. Past lives are but memories of our Soul’s journey. While we all expect to be seeing other loved ones when we cross; the memory of our life is kept alive only through those that knew you. A medium can access that memory of the essence of the soul, but it is only one memory of many lifetimes our essence experiences.

I hope that you can recognize yourself in the story as you grow into who you are to become. ~John

At four years old she loved animals. They seemed to know her. Who she is. They hold no judgment. Her eyes share an understanding. Her heart hears them speak. At ten she was shunned by her family. Made fun of and not invited to go along. Other siblings taking control. Her true friends are the animals. Unconditionally they give her strength. Unconditionally they give her the companionship and affection she desired.

She turned to them, sharing her secrets. Sharing her fears. They give her comfort. A hug to them represents a commitment. A lifetime of companions.

In her late teens she suffers. No friends to bind with. Everyone off in a different direction. Yet she hears them now, the animals of her life. They encourage her, befriend her. They listen to the fears of her mind, the ghosts of different life choices. One life created to hide behind. Her body has grown to protect her. To keep them away. Yet she suffers from the fear of being alone.

'Is this who I am?' she asks herself. 'Is this who I have become?' A thought of having a friend consumes her. Any friend that will care for me. 'I don't care anymore' her mind shouts. 'I need to escape, to explore, to finally be me'. Her mind triumphs her fears if even for a moment, only to be misguided, abused, left alone again. 'Why is this happening?' The hatred and cursing echo in her emotions and fears. 'Why is this me?' she cries. 'Why have I failed, why am I alone?'

'Get Out!' she shouts. She drives within, hiding to protect her heart. 'What lesson has my Soul presented me?' she asks herself.

She returns to her friends and the animals, and to try to find the lost companion that the partnership dissolved. Something inside her, a void has been growing. Training to learn to listen, she becomes a new healer in this part of her lifetime. She becomes a 'light~worker'. She sees others of like light and is drawn to them. She can 'sense' the feelings of others. Empathic and intuitive, she begins to hear the animals speak to her.

Her path changes to follow a light within. Small, it holds warmth. It feels familiar. She works hard to escape the past. She looks around to see the animals watching her. They begin to applaud her for the choices she is making. Her heart becomes filled like never before. Happiness fills her. She is given purpose for the first time in her life. She begins to see the inner light of others.

Wondering who these lights are, she chooses to embrace them. New Souls abound around her. One, a new shy Soul has taken a form in a man. He is a listener. He can touch her heart with a small look. A new flame within her ignites to show her a new step in her path. Familiar he feels, 'I've felt this before. So long ago'. 'Where have you been?' her Soul asks. Her fears subside and a new partnership takes hold.

'Companion' she feels 'with trust'. Many days turn to years. A longing, a void within, still there from the past. 'Still I do not know who I am'. She thinks of the ego, the 'what if's' in her life. Good choices and not so good. 'What if's' are the past, only showing a possibility that no longer exists. But saying 'what is' requires her to stand up for her thoughts and her beliefs.

No one to blame, no judgments but her own. Fears peek around each corner. Fears from the past reignite the thoughts. 'It is her choice', the Soul says, 'Her choice to take a fear. It will be a lesson for her. It will show her why she is given these gifts of compassion and love. It will show her how she can be a person of greatness, to share the messages from our animal friends and others.

She will embrace her gifts and share them with others. She will know the fear she chooses. She will look for the gifts the fears bring. 'Alone?' a flickering thought passes by. She sees the new friends she has made. They are there to hold her, to help her rise to her new her. They all want her to succeed. To be the person she can be.

'Take strength in this moment', the Soul shares. 'It will feed your faith. Look past the fears into the light the others carry. You will see the 'bling' inside each of them. You will care for each Soul'.

She will never be alone. She just needs to ask and remember who she is.

She stood at the top of a hill, looking down into the meadow below. Spotted trees dot the landscape. Jasper knew what lay ahead for her. She must check every tree for her Spirit, the tribal wizard had explained. Trees carry the essence of the world and the memories of lifetimes. They are the observers, the watchers of this world. Each listens to each other, sharing these memories. Our path leads us to listen to them for the history of our souls. These memories are only part of her Soul's eternal journey. Other worlds exist to experience as the choice of the Soul is driven to live.

Grand stories in her youth told of a storms that traveled up the valley. They always seemed to travel on the far end. This one was coming up the side they were on. Darkness from the clouds created a fear and anxiety within her. 'I hear the thunder but it's the lightning that creates my fears' Jasper said to herself, as lightning crashes thunder rolls down the valley. Hurrying back, she looked around their lodge to see if everyone was there. There were only eight people in her tribe. Everyone seemed to be there except Keenyon, her brother. Keenyon always disappeared when he should be with the group.

At fourteen summers, she had not been as tall as the rest of the group. She measured just short of ten hands of her small frame. Jasper had let her hair grow below her waist. Naturally brown, her hair had turned streaky blonde from the sun. Her long hair blew in the wind.

Keenyon was her younger brother. Well, not really her brother. While moving the camp eight summers ago, they had found him along the shores of the big lake up north. He was only about 5 summers old when he joined the camp. Now he had grown taller than Jasper in just two summers. He always hung by her. They were true friends. They would share stories and secrets to each other. The others left them alone as their bond grew stronger. Keenyon would tell her he could see plants as they grow and what they would look like in the fall. His eyes were bright green like a cats eyes. They would sneak out of the lodge together at night to look at the stars. He would point to them and tell her which one had her name and which ones held her future. They would tumble and play in the tall grasses. Keenyon would hide and Jasper could sense with her mind where he was. 'How do you do that', he'd always ask. 'I just know' she'd respond. Then he would grab her and tickle her until she begged to be let go and happy tears rolled down her face.

Jasper watched as three summers had passed. Keenyon was learning to survive. They had traveled far in the last few months. Their band had slipped to only six. A woman with three children, herself, Keenyon and one other. An older man who was the healer. At night he would disappear. No one asked where he went, only to see him again each morning. He seemed to 'see' with his eyes closed. His eyes were penetrating. It looked as though he could see through you. Darkness did not bother him.

A few days ago, he woke Jasper from her sleep. Not making any noise, they quietly left the group. He had rarely spoken to her but it seemed she knew what he intended for them. She followed him down into a small ravine. The trees were different here, she thought. The healer smiled at her. He always did that to her. Just smiled at her. Jasper liked him. His name was Mico. His skin was dark from the sun, hands rough from the work of the day. Standing next to a tree with red bark and was truly the tallest tree Jasper had seen, he spoke.

'The trees are Spirits. Each carries the story of their Soul and the life times they have witnessed. They reach upwards into the heavens of the universe. What you do not see, I see. They have a connection to the forever. A connection that binds them together, a connection that leads to the same source. 'It matters not which tree we speak to. We speak to all when we speak to one'. Jasper understood. She had wondered often about the trees.

Mico asked Jasper to touch the tree and listen. Jasper touched the rough red bark and closed her eyes. Wild images of seeing things from the ground level. Animals that had brushed against it. Fire in the distance and fear. 'Fear?' she asked Mico. 'The trees carry the same components that make you. All the feelings you have, a tree can share. While they look different from us, they experience the events that come their way. The only difference is they are forced to experience the event; they cannot turn and walk away as we can. Jasper felt despair. Even though the trees could not move, they have community. Their trunks, like arms, reach out to be held, to touch a fellow soul. The wisdom they carry is always pure. Guidance is what they offer to us. Companionship is what they desire.

When in your travels in life, ask the tress for guidance. Ask them to help point the way, for they know the true path of all souls'. They thanked the trees for this special moment and returned to the lodge.

Thinking of Keenyon. 'Should I go find him?' she thought, and was startled when a bolt of lightning hit nearby. She crawled to the door of the lodge. The wind now carried heavy pellets of rain. The rain water matted her hair to her face and made her squint her eyes to be able to see. She could not see across the compound. 'I hope Keenyon is safe' as she closed her eyes and turned back into the lodge. They had built their lodge next to a cliff, giving protection from the sun in the heat of the afternoon. Here the wind would not be straight as it curved up the side of the valley, twisted by the overhanging features of the cliff. The protrusions of overhanging stone caused the wind to roll faster and faster as it approached them up the valley. Jasper sat by the door and pulled her knees up to her chest and hung on. The others gathered on the opposite side of the lodge. Clustered together they felt safe.

She remembered cool evenings when the stars drifted across the sky. Jasper remembered her dream from years before. Three summers had come and gone, still her dreams took its toll on her sleep. Restlessness filled her when she closed her eyes. More separation of the people she knew. Their small group had continued to dwindle. Barely surviving, the elders gone from the cold last winter, choices had to be made to stay where they knew the area or to move on to new lands. They had talked about following the end of summer birds. They always returned in the spring full of life. They talked about moving. They could live with them in the warmer wintering areas, many miles and days away. Could they find a place to hunt food? Be in a safe place from other groups? Could they be in a place they could call home and not be alone? To allow a chance for their numbers to grow again, to feel comfort. Jasper laughed at herself. How many times had she thought of the same things. How many times did she ask for answers but was heard in her heart, 'Now you know'. Jasper had made a joke of that statement, not caring anymore what it could mean. Not wondering anymore where it had come from. She had thought she remembered that the message had come from Keenyon. Now she wasn't sure anymore. Had she just created it to satisfy another someone inside her?

She knew of the ‘someone’ inside her. Her Great Elder had spoken of it. It dug with a shovel in the bottom of her belly. It brought with it toxins of the past. Jasper wondered about the past. Her skin glistened, not like the others. Her eyes, blue like the sky with an amber star pattern. Always her eyes were deep in searching. She sometimes thought she would see a picture of another place. Here but not here. Images of people that would walk through her. But she could not feel them. Her eyes reflected what she saw in others. They seem to have the power to see through you. ‘Your eyes know the truth’, everyone said.

Jasper had grown taller the last three summers. Her back strong and willing. She was always there to help. Always gave her best. At night she also knew. She knew the thoughts of others. She felt the emotions of others. Sometimes Jasper had to hide. Hide her emotions from others. Hide her heart and desires from others. She was protecting herself, she thought. In the morning they were moving. In the morning a new adventure was beginning. They would not return here. They would leave the memories here with other failures.

Jasper began to look at life as a doubtful journey. ‘Why are we here? Who am I? Why do I exist?’

Suddenly the ground shook when a lightning bolt hit the top pole of the lodge. Jasper watched in horror as she saw the lightning travel down the center beam of the lodge and into the ground. Her family all suddenly became rigid as flames of fire burst forward and totally engulfed that end of the lodge. Jasper stood quickly to help them only to be pushed backwards out the door with a force of an explosion. Jasper clearly flew nearly 30 feet before being slammed to the ground. More horror overtook her as her eyes focused through the wind and rain to see the lodge be hit again by lightning. The lodge was blown apart. Nothing remained. It was totally vaporized by the heat from the blast.

She did not feel safe here. Other storms had come up the valley but this one had a different smell, a different feeling. Jasper closed her eyes and wished the storm would go away. She ran to an outcropping to get out of the wind and rain. The ozone smell stung her nostrils. Large boulders had fallen from the shaking of the ground caused by the lightning. Frightened, she felt something touch her leg. She looked down to see a hand with bloody fingers. She looked to find her brother. Lying under several huge stones, a pool of blood had formed under him. His fingers no longer moved. 'NO, NO, NO' she screamed at the sky. Gone, all gone. She had planned on leaving with her brother. Leaving with the family. Tomorrow she was leaving. Now she was setting out on her own journey . . . alone.

She was alone. Tears of the pain of loss overtook her. Whatever she thought of brought tears. She cried for what seemed to be hours. Her energy drained away with more tears. When she looked up the clouds were parting and the sun began to shine an eerie glow about the camp. Exhausted, Jasper stood to survey the camp area. Flattened, the entire camp gone. She began to try to remove the boulders off of Keenyon. Most were too big for her small frame to budge. She reached down and touched her brothers exposed hand. 'Be at peace my brother. I will see you again when this lifetime for me is complete'. She almost envied Keenyon, as he was now with his own people. She felt a kiss on her cheek, a thought of Keenyon and the bond they had. Her family had survived many generations. Now they were gone.

The sun disappeared behind more dark clouds just before dusk. Sounds in the distance echo down the valley, the remains now of distant thunder. Creatures of all types were returning after the storm and began sounding their disapproval of the oncoming darkness. Darkness creeps into the skin and brings coolness and a new awareness. Sometimes she wondered if the darkness really existed. 'Maybe it is just my mind that goes to sleep', she thought.

Jasper walked slowly over the camp grounds. She had lost all of her clothing except for what she wore. Picking up items that she thought might be useful, she found a shirt and foot coverings. Though not hers, she tried them for fit. The shirt a little big, the foot coverings just right. She found her little bag of secrets. A bag made of an animal skin, similar to a fox. The red color made it easy to say who it belonged to. She carried a blue crystal she found in a cave three summers ago. It seemed to glow in the darkness of night. A length of hide six times her height left over from a hunt. A flat black stone with a sharp edge. Fish hooks made from bone. Some fine cloth the old woman had made and a hardened rib cage from a fish that she used to get tangles out of her hair. She also picked up a small hide from an animal. She attached the hide over her shoulders and felt the warmth of the animals' soul refresh her.

Jasper knelt and clutched her small bag of possessions. She did not look back as she walked in the darkness. No one would see that she was not there. 'There is nothing to keep me here' Jasper whispered to herself. Her brother gone, she held back a sniffle and a frown. She was alone now. A choice presented to her. She wanted to learn, to be more. The others just existed. Day to day. The same. 'Not Me' Jasper told herself. 'Not me, ever!'

Jasper walked silently down the path towards the valley she had taken many times before. She did not look back.

After what seemed a long time, stumbling on roots and stones that crossed the path in the faint light, she came to a small clearing. Jasper and her brother had stopped there many times to look at the stones that seemed to bulge out of the ground. Bright red stones, like flames coming out of the ground. He would say they are the fire in my heart. Jasper caught the tear dropping off her chin.

As Jasper sat on the largest stone, memories of Keenyon came to her mind. The bond that she had with him. The whistle he would make when he was looking for her. Both Jasper and Keenyon had a tendency to disappear from the group. She would never really go anyplace; more like just would fade out. Jasper would feel like she was in a mist. A quiet, cool place where she could be alone. Jasper used this 'away time' to think. She always thought of her life. Seeing the way other people lived and wondered how they existed. What purpose did each carry with them? Where would this journey of life lead them? 'HEY', where am I going?'

When Keenyons' whistle came, she 'popped' back to this reality. No one ever asked where she was. It's as if she was in both places at the same time.

Jasper heard a whisper in her ear. She knew that voice. How could it be? It was her brother, Keenyon. 'Soon you will know' he said. He repeated the words, the whisper sounding like the wind. She stood up and slowly looked around her. She made a large circle around the red stone. The wind seemed to always be in her face. The direction she faced did not matter.

Then suddenly all was silent. Nothing. Total quiet engulfed her. The strong wind was gone. There is something in the air. Something more frightening than the lightning, thunder or of falling stones. None had ever seen this before. A light in the sky. Not a star or one of the two moons. The light, glimmering and centered on the far side of the valley below. It dropped fast at first from the sky then slowly as it grazed the tall grasses, then seemed to settle to the ground.

The winds seem to pick up again and she had to close her eyes to keep the flying dust out. She suddenly had a feeling of someone touching her. A weird feeling. Not of hands but of a wrap around her. Her legs held tight together and her arms held tight, pressed along her sides. She tried to open her eyes to see who or what it was that held her, but could not. Her body became rigid. The force holding her became stronger the more she tried to move. Fear gripped her as she felt lifted off the ground. As her body was held immobile, her mind raced. She did not feel that she was in danger. Her mind started to reach out. She had the power to sense her surroundings. In her mind's eye she saw that she was in a silver colored cylinder of light, though not solid to the touch of her mind. She could feel the cylinder hold her but could not feel any bindings.

An overwhelming feeling of relaxation and joy overcame her. Her body quit feeling any contact. It was a floating feeling, yet she had no feeling of being lifted. Her mind seemed to drift out of her body. As she rose above her physical self, her inner sight became aware of her surroundings. She saw her body below her. Her body straight and firm, held in the light cylinder. 'Soon you will know' again went though her head. She could feel the presence of Keenyon but could not see him. She felt as if she were a cloud, mixing with the wind.

What an odd feeling of seeing herself yet aware of her brother and the activity around her. She wanted to laugh. She felt as if she was holding her breath. Her lungs released her breath with a rush which was odd because she was not in her body. She started to laugh. The loudest she could muster was a whoosh in her mind. Her smile went ear to ear. 'What is going on?' she thought.

She watched from above as the light in the cylinder darkened. She could not see any light. Total darkness. She could not sense her body any longer. Jasper focused on her mind. 'I am here, I am real', she said to herself.

'Soon you will know'

'Soon you will know'

Jasper was in wonderment. The feelings she was sensing seemed to be within her, then the same feelings would come from all around her. Emotions, thoughts, imagination all came from the same place. She tried to see herself but could not. She imagined herself as a ball of light. No boundaries held her. Her beams of light reaching out to touch, to feel the universe around her. She thought of Keenyon. A whiff of sadness washed over her and was gone. In her minds heart she now felt complete.

She looked for her physical body and could not find it. Again she heard, 'Soon you will know'. As she existed someplace where no time existed she began to see others. Small balls of light, hundreds, and then thousands, much like herself. Now more than she could imagine. Filling her. 'Home' she thought. They were rushing to meet her. Exuberance and joy filled her. She felt happy and complete. No fear existed in this thought.

More than she ever felt as the other lights came close to her she seemed to know 'who' or 'what' they were. They were like me, she thought. They are me! She watched as a path cleared between them. In front of her, selected balls of light centered themselves in a line down the center of the path. They floated inline, some having a larger gap between them than others. She turned her mind behind her and saw a similar line of light balls. This line seemed longer that the other. More space between them. Jasper nudged her mind forward getting close enough to touch the light closest to her. 'Familiar' Jasper thought. 'Where have I seen you before? Have we met before?'

Jaspers' mind froze. No thought could be created. Jasper's mind just watched. What appears to be the image of others, they were of her. Different clothing, different hair color. Different gender. All seemed different but she knew they were of the same essence. Places she had seen and not seen. Skies of different colors. Sometimes Jasper felt she was a male. Other times a mother, a brother, a sister, or father. A scene appeared before her of things she could never imagine. The sky was not quite blue, more maroon in color. Three moons hovered in the sky. The air not as crisp as she remembered. More like a smell of a carcass that had been in the sun too long though no animals existed here. The ground sputtered gases into the air. Above, a cylinder like the one she remembered her body was being held. A stream of particles formed a cloud as they escaped from the cylinder and disappeared. Looking at the ground again movement is seen as molecules combine. Just one word sounded in her mind, 'creation' she heard.

It seemed an eternity as she watched the place below her evolve. She watched two of the moons collide, sending particles to the surface with a flaming tails. Over the millennium, the two broken moons formed into one. The surface covered with unusual vegetation, purple in color.

Jasper's essence moved out to a place in space. Time still zoomed forward. Watching from a distance, small lights scattered around the planet popped into existence. Soon large groupings of lights grew from nothing. Floating lights appeared above the centers of lights. Streaks of fire burst from the floating lights and traveled into the depths of the universe, disappearing almost instantly.

Jasper's feelings became more intense. Every molecule of her being vibrated. Her light seemed to be changing. She felt a little anxiety with these new feelings. After just getting used to the new her, this change made her feel different. As she changed, her light seemed to be getting smaller, while the others remained the same size. She felt pressure, like she was being pushed into a small container.

She struggled against the pressure.

She felt trapped. 'Why am I feeling this, what is happening?' she asked herself. Smaller and smaller she felt. The pressure was so intense. Her light, now crushed, begged to be let out. The more she struggled the more her fear grew. The fear of being alone. Objects in space were being drawn toward her. Emotions filled her. Every fear she had experienced and knew jumped to the front of her thoughts. Everyone, everything, putting a strangle hold on her. Tighter and tighter, her light screamed to be let out but could not escape.

She felt she could not breathe. She was alone.

Nothing existed around her.

Absolute nothingness.

Terribly alone. Her thoughts existed of the life she had been experiencing. Her thoughts existed of Keenyon and her family. Her memory of this lifetime was special to her. Now she wondered, doubted them to be true.

The black of nothingness touched her and she wanted to scream. She began to doubt herself more. Was she really here? Was she really, truly lost? What is the nothingness that seems to feed on her fears? Her essence searched for an answer. The black of nothingness enveloped her small, infinitesimal light. No, there was no light left in her. No, light wasn't the correct 'being' word. Essence is more correct. An essence is a spirit, the fundamental nature of all things. A feeling of exuberance filled her.

Suddenly her essence was released to become. Become what she had begun to become. To just be! Clouds of stars surrounded her. The nothing of space was now filled with everything. Things she did not know. Things she remembered. Things that keep her in awe of existing. An essence! I know now. I am still Jasper, but I am not. I exist, but do not exist. 'I am the essence of myself!' she proclaimed. 'Of who I am'.

Jasper felt an explosion release inside her and her release sent light particles to fill the universe. Stardust stuck to her and became her. She felt born into a new life, a new experience. Jaspers' light filled the universe and the night sky. Keenyon whispered to her 'Soon you will know'. Her thoughts were everywhere, and nowhere at the same time. Just knowing, everything. Jasper grasped for a deep breath. The bonds that held her body tight loosed just a bit. Jasper opened her eyes. With a start, she saw she was lying next to the red stone. Memories filled her. Yes, the storm had been real.

Yes, the lodge was gone with her family. Keenyon was dead, killed by falling boulders. No one to hold her. Alone. Jasper felt lost, alone and in a daze. She wondered if what she was remembering true or not. She heard a whisper, 'Now you know'. 'What do I know?' she asked herself. Jasper stood slowly. Wobbly on her legs, her mind began to clear. She looked down the valley. The strange light was gone. The morning sun felt good on her face. Looking around the base of the red stone she found her bag of treasures.

She took a step forward and slipped. The ground was still wet from the storm. Her clothing clung to her. She must have slipped in the darkness and hit her head. Her hand touched a sore spot on the side of head her head. 'Was all this real?' she questioned herself. Jasper felt uneasiness in her abdomen. Feeling like she had eaten too many berries, but also feeling a huge void at the same time. The uneasiness turned into cramping and she had to jump off the red stone and run into the brush as the berries she had eaten earlier hastened to return to the ground. 'YUK'

Taking a deep breath, she sat back onto the red stone. Jasper pushed off the red stone and started down the path to go deeper into the valley. Jasper passed more berries as she walked. This time she just collected only a few and placed them in her bag. She spied a wild veggie growing along the path. Pulling it from the ground, she rubbed the dirt off and ate. The veggie tasted great compared to all the berries she had eaten. Almost the texture of an apple, but softer and not as sweet. The valley was always rich in food this time of late summer. She continued slowly as the path drifts left and right, slowing going to the bottom of the valley. Tall grass began to hide her view of her direction. She knew these paths well and it wasn't long until she came to the stream. The stream cut the valley in half. Jasper sat by its edge to rest. Finding her shadow, she knew it was only late morning. Again the thoughts of last night and the memories she retained filled her mind. Jasper closed her eyes as she imagined the stardust that had covered her. It was the one time in her life that she was not afraid to be alone, but strong and courageous.

She felt comforted by the compassion she felt. The memory brought joy to her heart. Jasper took off her clothing and stepped into the stream. The mud and dust had caked onto her skin. Using the fine sand at the bottom of the stream she washed herself and cleaned her clothing. She skin felt fresh and glistened in the sun light. Her light clothing she wore was almost dry when she put it on. Refreshed, she gathered her bag and crossed the stream.

The tall grass seemed not as tall on this side of the stream she noticed. Bare spots became easy to pick out and made her crossing the valley floor easier. As she neared the wall of the valley, she noticed a large bird circling overhead. It appeared to be eyeing her as if she was its next meal. 'Follow or lead my friend' she yelled up to the bird. It listened and barked a loud screech, dipped its wings at her and dived passed her. Jasper almost had to duck from being hit, but the bird was an acrobatic master. Jasper felt the wind from its wings mess her hair. 'Hey, be nice' she exclaimed to the bird. Another screech came from the bird. 'Okay, you lead' as she picked up her pace to keep the bird in sight. The wing span of the bird was easily eight times her length in hands. The magnificent golden brown feathers touched the air and created a majestic lift. The bird sensed the currents of air along the valley wall and seemed to fall upwards.

Once Keenyon had told her that he could see out of a bird's eye, to look at the ground from above. 'That would be a great present' she thought. Moving too fast to close her eyes while half walking and half running to keep pace with the bird, she committed to trying that when she was sitting down during her next rest time. It seemed only a short time and she was aware that the bird had led her to a place in the wall that reached up and out of the valley. In the summers that they had been there, Jasper had never ventured this far from the lodge before.

Jasper picked her way around some rocks and stopped. There, reflecting the sun light were numerous stones. They came in many colors. As she picked up one of each color she could feel each stone humming at her. Each color vibrated a little different from the next. 'They have the colors of a bright rainbow' Jasper said to herself. She palmed the stones and when they touched all together she felt them send a gentle jolt of energy up her arm and throughout her body in the smallest fraction of time stiffening her body. They tingled her right to the cellular level, to her core. She separated the stones and placed each into her bag, making sure they did not touch each other. 'Wow' that was enjoyable she thought as she again started walking up the crevasse the bird had lead her. There were dark areas in the crevasse she steered away from. Not afraid, just cautious of where she was walking. She had no length of measurement to describe how long the climb took.

She just kept going. Some places were easier than others. She had to climb over boulders that blocked her climb. Just as she was beginning to wonder if she would ever emerge, she looked up to see the bird resting at the plateau in front of her. It seemed to be clawing at the dirt at its feet. When she got closer she could see that the bird was eating small bugs the size of her big toe and didn't stop until they were gone. She remembered seeing these bugs at the lodge. Their bite could make you sick. She remembered a young girl that was bitten repeatedly where she had lain down to nap. She did not wake up. The bugs' bite had put her into a deep sleep, then death. The bird cackled at her once and took off. 'Thank you' she loudly spoke. That could have been a nasty sight. 'I suppose you should have a name as I see you as being the largest and proudest bird and a protector as well, I shall call you Como'.

What was she thinking, naming a bird? A large golden brown feathered hunter. He has fierce claws, but could muster a smile if you looked close enough to the corners of his hooked beak. His beak and claws were stained red from the blood of his victims. He landed near her on a thick branch from a downed tree. She remembered her visit to the trees with Mico. 'I wonder if the downed trees can hear me?' she thought. Jasper stepped slowly towards the giant bird. 'Gentle, gentle', she thought out loud wanting to make sure the bird could hear her thoughts. Como lowered his massive head as she drew near. Jasper slipped a berry into her hand and slowly reached to offer the fruit to the bird. Como jerked his head up and looked her square into her eyes. There was no fear in his gaze, only being inquisitive and compassionate. Jasper saw what looked like a tear in the corner of his eye. 'You have a funny smell' Como announced in her mind.

Now that really shook Jasper. Her hand dropped the berry and she stepped back. 'You shall have no fear of me' Como commanded. Jasper leaned forward thinking she did not hear what she heard. 'Do not fear me creature. In my presence you will bow to no one and fear nothing. I am the king of the skies. I seek only to serve creatures that see life from the heart. I have been watching you for years, since you were small. The colors around you tell me you are pure of heart and you are a healer. We seek the same goal. We seek the same path. Yours is just stuck to the ground'.

Jasper lost her stance at those remarks and landed smartly on her butt.

Her adventure had begun. Jasper held the sides of her face, elbows on her knees and smiled at him. 'You remind me of someone I knew not long ago. He spoke the same words to me. I can still hear his ruff voice speak to me', she said laughingly, remembering Mico. Como responded with 'And I shall be your friend. We travel together'. With that Como jumped up from his perch and lifted into the sky. He circled overhead and pointed the way for Jasper.......

Two suns later, Jasper felt tired. She had not eaten anything solid, not since the veggies in the valley. The strength in her legs seemed diminished and they ached. Her mind could not focus. 'Como", she tried to send with her mind. He had not been seen for the last full day. Alone, though she knew her direction, she did not have ambition to continue at his pace. Como surprised her by being behind her with no sound. Jasper was startled and laughed at the same time. 'COMO' she yelled in a half fright. After her are heart rate returned to normal, Jasper asked, 'Where we going? Como explained that the world was getting smaller each sun cycle.

The land they stood on had been shaking for the last two days. Dry land was becoming un-survivable. Heat from the world seeped out in several locations. Animals of all types where traveling in the same direction. "There is an energy or force that is drawing me to the middle of the group of animals. I have traveled for almost a day to find its center but could not'.

The sun was settling and Jasper was astonished at seeing the edges of the sun leap out to lick the space around it. In this light and angle just at the horizon, the sun was strange, and not the same color she remembered and looked larger, almost angry. These sights had not been seen in her lifetime. They rested together. Como tucked his wings tight to him and settled to the ground. He too had spent energy and needed rest. Jasper knelt next to him and felt his strong feathers. She groomed the length of several feathers, feeling the life they contained. She had never held a bird before and the feeling was astonishing. 'Como?' Jasper offered. 'Where will we go? I do not feel alone when you are near me, but I fear tomorrow'. Como said softly in her mind as he closed his eyes to rest, 'I too am in wonder of tomorrow. I do not feel safe in this world. I have not found any others like me. The animals, few remain, few seek the source, our center of our travels. We shall eat in the new sun and make haste to the end of the day. Now rest, for our journey has but begun'. Jasper felt secure in the touch of this large beast. Her breathing slowed as she entered a sleep of deep rest. She did not move all night, securely tucked in the feathers of Como.

The new sun brought with it a new feeling in her stomach. A cramp had developed low in her abdomen. She felt the pain shoot across hip to hip. 'OHHHH!' she exclaimed. Como jumped up and nearly tripped over Jasper. Como jumped into the air and was gone. In minutes he returned with a plant and asked Jasper to chew is slowly. It tasted sweet yet had a tang to it that made her mouth alive. She coughed lightly as the plants flavor increased even more. She could feel the juices in her mouth travel into her stomach. As she ate and swallowed more plant, her pain eased and her strength returned. 'Thank you' she shared with Como. Resting, Como said, 'This plant and many more will not survive here. These are healing plants. Your pain will not return'.

A pack of dogs could be heard in the distance. Their bark and howls signaled the pack to come together. They had found an animal that had fallen and had a broken leg. While the creature was moving slowly, it still has the instinct for survival. The dogs gathered and took turns taunting the animal. Two making a lunging motion for distraction, while two others leaped in to sink their jaws into its flesh. Strong jaw muscles held tight as the animal struggled to get free. They held tight. A third dog came forward and grabbed the animal by its throat. With a twisting and jarring motion a large piece of flesh came loose. Blood from a large vein spurted everywhere. The animal gurgled some sounds of defeat and went silent. Its' heart stopped beating. The life and soul left the animal, its eyes turning to a dull black.

The dogs had a field day, gorging themselves for the fresh flesh and meat. Como kept a watchful eye on the dogs. He knew of the beasts and had tasted them before. He did not like the taste of them but when hunting was scarce choose to dive and grab the animal with its huge claws across its back, keeping clear of its nipping teeth. Como would then climb to a height just short of the clouds and drop the animal. Como would then circle around the animal, as if taunting it, as it gained speed towards its end. Just before the ground, Como opened his wings and came to a quick hover. The prey now hit the ground hard, bounced once and was still.

Circling above, he sent Jasper the image that he saw. Jasper was resting, her abdomen feeling better, when the pictures from Como appeared in her mind. She felt as though she were riding Como's back. Looking down she saw herself not far from where she was. She noted the direction and opened her eyes. Jasper picked up her bag and stood up. The days walk/running had taken its toll on her legs. Her legs a little stiff, she looked down to see the fine cuts the grass blades had made on her calf's. Dried blood marked the spots. She shook off the feelings and moved toward the downed animal. Nearing the spot, she spied Como standing above the animal, his beak bright red. Como had scared the pack into the fields and hills around them and had been enjoying his meal. 'Please join me as this creature surely will have friends in the area and the dogs are still very close', he told her in her mind.

Jasper pulled the flat black stone from her bag as she knelt next to the carcass. The skilled hands cut the hide off to expose the muscles. A quick slice with the stone, she had her first taste of fresh meat for weeks.

Having her fill and sharing pieces of flesh she'd cut out with Como, she sliced several pieces and wrapped them in a piece of hide. She placed the meat into her bag and sat back. Her stomach full, she eyed Como. 'Where do you come from and where are we going?' she spoke to Como. 'HA', Como replied. He did not speak as she did but knew his words. 'I am from the other side of this place. It is cold most of the time with light snow and ice on the ground. We perch in the mountains high above. I am on a journey to seek the others of myself'.

'For many summers, I have been looking but have only found where they have been. The trail they leave is hard to follow but is following the birds of the end of summer'. Now Jasper said 'HA, that too is my journey'. Como commented, 'There are not many like me anymore. Once we had large numbers, but this place is not friendly. The animals that we hunt are but gone. Your small family is the last that I have seen in this valley. The surrounding plains and valleys do not hold more of you. I have crossed your path many times but have never seen others. Jasper was astonished and suddenly felt alone. Alone, sadness entered her heart.

Como continued, 'While you are very small, you may sit on my back. I am aware of your fears and will hold them for you'. Jasper reached into her bag and removed the cut length of hide she carried. Como lowered his head to allow Jasper to place it around his neck. Climbing up, Jasper felt his strong muscles in his neck. Seated behind his head on his shoulders, Jasper clinched her legs tight. Como smiled, knowing that the fear of falling was on the top of her list.

In two steps Como was off the ground and rising towards the clouds. The sun was shining brightly, not obstructed by the trees or by varying landscapes. The thin clouds provided a nice cool mist in Jaspers face. She became more and more comfortable the longer they stayed aloft. Como was kind not to do any acrobatics as she had seen him do before. Como interrupted her, 'The small friend I saw you with, what became of him and your family?' Jasper choked back the thought of Keenyon under the boulders. 'He and the family are gone. They all passed in the lightning storm'. Como replied with, 'I have known your friend many times. I could sense him in my mind and he could see what I saw. Just as you did when I sent you the pictures from above'. Jasper gasped in surprise. 'Keenyon was telling the truth!'

They both watched the sun disappear. Nighttime did not force Como to the ground. Gliding, Como outlined his journey to Jasper. He had watched this world for a hundred summers. The planet was at its end. While he wanted to continue in this existence, he did not know where he was headed. This new information puzzled Jasper. Her mind went deep into thought.

She began to remember the images when she left the camp for the last time. The beautiful universe that had formed around her. The small lights that formed a staggered line. 'Future lifetimes', Como offered as he could see her thoughts. The stardust had clung to her. In the faint light of the moons, she looked down at her arms. Sparkles of light glistened. She was covered by stardust! 'It was all real!' she exclaimed. The light in the valley, being held physically, her mind leaving her body. All the gorgeous forming of the universe. Then she had felt that she was but an essence. Reliving these images in her mind, her emotions flowed deep in sorrow mixed with the wonderment of becoming her own essence. Como turned his head and smiled at her.

'Yes, now you know' she heard in her mind. It was Keenyon, she recognized. Yes, Keenyon had become an essence as well!

In the view of the horizon ahead, shining in the darkness was a small point of light. A thin beam of light, energy, pointed to the sky, piercing the thin clouds and out into the void of space. The beam went on forever. As they neared the light it grew larger. Como drifted lower as they came closer. A strange feeling washed over them. Warm but without heat.

A small clearing near the light offered Como a place to touch the ground. Jasper slide from his back, holding her bag, and they both walked slowly towards the light. Astonished, they watched as a bright figure emerged from the light. Not physical, only it seemed to have form. It drifted over the ground towards them. The figure spoke to them in their minds. 'Clearly you are the ones. Clearly you both have the awareness to become who you are. I invite you to join me. This planet will cease to exist in a very short time. You are both welcome to continue your journey. The light you see behind me is a portal. A passage to where you want to go. It has no limitations. It is a doorway to your past and future. Your thoughts will guide you. I see you both as beings of light. You can travel together or each to what you seek. All you need to do is enter the light. The beam will do the rest. Como, you have desires of joining your kind. I honor you for that choice. Jasper, you want so much. You carry the past and future with you. The past has great memories, both joyful and painful. Your heart tells your story. You have a loss that runs deep within. 'You will not be alone'.

Jasper knew what the light-being meant. Her dreams and thoughts were always of Keenyon. She had always felt a bond, a connection to his soul. 'This lifetime does not hold your future. Your friend has shared this lifetime and many others in the past. He will also share many more in your future. He has spoken to you many times. That is why you are here. Many lifetimes ahead will be of companionship, of hope and comfort. Hardships will also follow. Thoughts of this lifetime you must remember. You will not always be the female and he the male. Roles change.

When you choose a future you will experience it from the conception of that lifetime. The memories of the past will be of future lifetimes, though the choices you will make will guide you to your friend'.

'The Stardust is your guide, your road map of existence. Like the lines on your hands that have formed from your choices, the Stardust offers a path. The blue crystal in your bag is the key to your life. Hold it now and feel the warmth it carries'. Jasper reached into her bag a retrieved the blue crystal. The seven other small stones came out with her other hand. 'What of these stones?' she asked the light being. 'These small crystals represent you, who you are. Each holds the energy of characteristics of this physical existence. They will change with your experiences. They will change with how you perceive things and who you become. They require balance. They will push and pull you to the choices that are offered. These are the tools of your Soul. The light inside the blue crystal glows with your life. The more brilliant it glows, the closer you will come to your purpose of that lifetime. Use this light in lifetimes that have many questions. Not all lifetimes carry your desire. Some lifetimes will seem to be a pleasure with no difficulties. Many more lifetimes will have challenges that can be overcome. These challenges will return in other future lifetimes until your choices lead you to find the answer to overcome those challenges'.

Como stepped forward toward the light. 'Jasper, I have you in my heart and will carry yours with me to my end. I know we will see each other again. My form may be different but you will know my Soul'. With that Como disappeared into the light. A burst of light formed a bulge that traveled at light speed upward toward the universe and was gone. 'You will know me', she smiled.

The 'light~being' stepped up to Jasper and reached out with a form of light similar to a hand. Jasper touched the light and her fears melted away. The light-being offered compassion and unconditional love as she was guided toward the light. 'How do I know where to go, which life to choose?' She asked. 'Let your heart and blue crystal guide you. When you look inside your heart the blue crystal will ignite. The brighter its blue light, the closer you are to your goal'. One more step forward and she was absorbed into the light. As she entered she saw her world begin to breakup, lightning strikes everywhere.

Jasper was not in a physical form. She had returned to be her essence. She too felt as light, like before. The colored stones of herself shed their hardness and became the light of each color. The blue crystal with its light glowing hovered at her center, the colored lights forming random orbits around the blue light. While traveling very fast, she could see the small balls of light that were her past and future physical opportunities. Her thoughts controlled her speed and she slowed to look at the first ball of light. She could sense being a male, tall and strong. 'No, not this lifetime', her heart light told her that Keenyon was not there and continued forward. She slowed at the next few lights and simply asked her heart if this one or that one was her fate. The blue light, not changing in its brilliance.

She remembered the light-being saying that it was all about choices to find her path. She felt happier than she ever had been. Full and complete. Jasper became anxious and chose the next lifetime. Jasper's energy entered the lifetime with little splash and disappeared within it.

This lifetime of Jasper contains the first emotions, fears, and learning of the body energy basics. Did you pick them up?
Crystals/Stones of different colors, the rainbow.
The colors represent our Chakra's. Each holding our personal characteristics at any given moment.
The blue crystal being center of the Soul.
Energy of thought; telepathy
Light-Beings
Animal Telepathy
Out-of-body experience
Communications with Spirit (Medium-ship)
Communications with Nature

Jasper was not Jasper anymore. She looked at her birth, a boy. While in the womb, she felt the warmness around her. Noises and voices surrounded her. Music filled her. Life seemed to go smoothly. 'This lifetime I am Thomas' the essence of the Soul nudged her. Thomas grew and experienced a great family. They traveled; he learned the history of this place and that. This world carried many beautiful things. Thomas became a businessman that was sought after for his skill at negotiations.

Thomas though did not feel complete. He searched for a partner, a Soul Mate to share with. His trials at friendships ended poorly, leaving him alone. He always felt a void within himself. He studied religions and became fluent in their policies and prophecies'. He was welcomed into all religions, though none filled his void. He met a woman that shared his thoughts, shared his mind. He offered to share his soul and they became wed and produced few children.

During his travels with his family, Thomas always thought he had been to a place before. Not knowing how he felt that way or when that could have happened, he buried these happenstance inside him. One day while in his later years he spoke with his spouse about this. 'Déjà vu, it's called', his wife said. His eyes opened wider at hearing the strange word and started to search for an answer to this.

On his next business trip, a friend he had shared some of his feeling, with had recommended a 'seer' with a great reputation. Thomas had chance to visit this 'seer'. Though he was alone on this trip, he felt curious to find his path and his answers and planned a day away from his busy schedule. The morning sun was bright as he let out on his journey. He had a drive of several hours before his encounter. He had time to think of all the questions that had raced through his mind for years. When nearing the location of the 'seer', he noticed the foliage become thicker, not able to see far ahead down the winding road. He slowed as the trees created darkness, an eerie feeling covered him. Anxiety made his heart race in anticipation of his meeting.

Thomas arrived early in the afternoon and entered the small shack surrounded by exotic flowers. He stood still, smelling their essence. Entering, he looked at the four corners and the eclectic grouping of articles, statues, and other collectables that filled the shelves. Books and reading cards spread throughout. A small table and chair in the corner invited him to sit. A small woman older seemed to appear out of nowhere. She said, 'I am from the past, live in the present and see the future. What are you looking for from me Thomas?' Shocked, Thomas said, 'How do you know me?' 'I am Lillie, and I have seen you come to me this day. You feel alone, but have been here before, many times, many lifetimes ago'. Thomas moved to the edge of his chair, his hands became damp and sweat beads formed on his brow.

'I do not know why I am here. It is said that I experience Déjà vu, though I am not sure what that means. I do not understand how you know my name, as we have never met'. Thomas announced.

Lillie responded with, 'Yes, in this lifetime we have not physically met. You have been a great grandson to me in a lifetime before this. Everyone you meet is part of your history. Everyone you've met, your Soul has met before. Everyone you will meet holds part of who you are. A feeling of being some place before only validates your path. Your choices in this lifetime have made changes for where you are in this moment. You are repeating several lessons, to come to solution, to choose differently from previous life experiences'.

Thomas asked, 'Is this why I feel so alone? I have a feeling of being not from here, or wherever I go. I meet people and they feel different from me. I have been seeking a partner. Though I am married, I feel there is more. I always dream of the same woman and I don't know who or where she is. I am happy at home, but feel there is more'. Thomas held his head in a shameful way. Listening to this 'seer', Thomas was eager to learn more. 'You are from a distant galaxy, a different world that no longer exists. Yours is an old Soul, one that has repeated many lifetimes. You are choosing the wrong path to freedom and will allow for more choice for your next lifetime. You like the successes this life has provided to you. So you repeat it. There is a soul that searches for you as well. One that holds the key to your progression. Thomas was amazed at what he was hearing. He had studied the religions and faiths of the world but none speak of the Soul this way. ‘How do I find her?’ he asked. ‘Soon you will know’ Lillie whispered as she faded and disappeared before his eyes.

Shaken by what he had witnessed, Thomas felt lost and alone. The little shack became cold. Again he tested his mind to the words the ‘seer’ had spoken. ‘Soon you will know’. He repeated them again and again. Darkness was still far away when he emerged from the shack. He noticed it was very late afternoon.

Driving slowly and making his way back to the hotel, a storm kicked up. Hardly out of the forest, dark clouds hovered overhead. Gentle rain at first as the winds increased. Then the clouds released their fury in a solid downpour of rain making it hard to see out the windshield. Lightning started to flash around him and he nervously continued down the narrow road. He looked for shelter along the road as the rains filled the air. Ahead, a hollow to the right, contained a cave. He stopped the car and ran to its protective opening. Just as he was about to enter, a bolt of lightning hit the top of the entrance and large stones fell and crushed him. ‘I know’ he whispered to himself. The essence of Thomas’

Soul hovered over him then vanished. Thomas' body was not found for three days. His family wept at the loss of their beloved.

Though Thomas is Jasper in this lifetime, she re-experienced the death and crossing as her brother Keenyon had in their first lifetime.

The Void within is the driving force within us to seek fulfillment.

Crossing over; the Soul leaving the physical

Psychic Gypsies, Tarot readings

Déjà vu; being somewhere that feels you've been there before.

Past-Life Soul partners, Soul-mates

'Jasper' 'No, that doesn't sound or feel like my name, not anymore', as she pondered the next few light lifetimes. Her essence reflected on what she had just learned. In her heart she looked for Keenyon. In her true essence, she was challenged by what she knew.

She had learned to slow down before entering a lifetime. Do I have to start at conception? A picture formed for her of her parents 'to be' and the possibilities that they would offer her. It did give her a chance to look at her family, to make a choice of who they might be and who she would become. Suddenly her heart, or what her heart might feel like, created an anxiety that she had not felt before. Her blue light inside her pulsed rapidly. Yes, this is my lifetime that she may reunite with Keenyon. She slowed to look at the lifetime in front of her and entered the light. Her conception was exciting. Her birth painful. Her first breath and early childhood. Loss of family in an accident caused by a lightning storm echoed from emotions in the past. She felt alone.

Alone again in her late teens just as in lifetimes before. Here in this lifetime travel was in vehicles that floated in the air, then zipped through the air seemingly knowing where it was going. The buildings bright and shiny. Many were pinnacles that reached into the sky. Her home is in the building on the left and had automatic doors. Instant food preparation and many comforts. School was a blast. Her friends all reached for the same goals. No one different in stature or structure. All learned the same basic lessons, personal growth was encouraged. Physically her body was attractive, at least that what the boys would say. Caitlyn is her name in this lifetime. Pale blue eyes with amber star shaped centers around the pupils, medium brown hair with golden streaks. She was not all that popular at school except for a few people. When she graduates next month she would set off, by herself.

She always felt a desperate void within her. A feeling of not being complete. She had lived with an aunt who had been very successful in her business. Caitlyn never wanted anything. If she dreamt it, her aunt would provide except for one thing. Caitlyn had dreams that no one could provide an answer for her as to where the dreams came from or what the nighttime dreams meant. They were of a small girl, living on a different world. Barely existing and alone. When the dreams came to view her future they would abruptly end. These dreams repeated nightly, sometimes for weeks. She felt depressed. No one to share her dreams with, she buried them within her.

Her friends at school became excited as graduation day was finally here. Caitlyn shared in their joy and smiles, knowing that she would be gone the following day. Her plans made, packed and ready to go. She had planned on searching, to fill the void within. She knew of her path. She had seen it several times in her mind. She wanted to expand her exposure to the truth around her. Her desires drove her but they were different from her friends. She had not been too popular with her goals and did not share them often. One friend, Betty, had invited her to visit a fortune teller. 'Ya, right' Caitlyn thought. 'Like, he knew where I was going after graduation!' Betty proclaimed.

Not far from her home, it took only 20 minutes to arrive at the door of the psychic. Betty was excited. She had seen this psychic before and was very thrilled at the information she received. The 'Teller' had told her of her school, her boyfriend, ex-boyfriend, family. The 'Teller' also said she would go to Europe to take specialized training in bio-chemistry. Betty has always interested in the inner sciences. Caitlyn would not have any of that. She preferred to exercise her mind. She had taken a special class in meditation and had found some calmness there when she would go within.

The door opened and a middle aged man looked around the edge of the door. 'Betty! How good to see you again. You and your friend, come in!' Caitlyn followed her friend into a small room setup for doing his work. It had been about 14 months since Betty had been here. Betty also noticed that the room hadn't changed. The man introduced himself to Caitlyn, 'Hello, my name is Crisp. He relayed a story of his youth that his mother always loved the way he would tuck in his shirt to keep it straight, crisp. The kind of nickname that stuck with you for your life. Crisp liked it as it reminded him of his family and his special bond with his Mother.

Crisp explained that he was telepathic with his Mother. She was a special person as well. Gifted in many skills, she could always tell where Crisp was. They'd play games of hide and seek, yet she always would find him. Crisp also explained that her faith had led them down many different paths, each having a lesson for him. She had passed about 10 years earlier. Crisp said that she also visited quite often in spirit and they still have lengthy conversations. Her message to him is always ended with 'I am happy and well and that I will always be with you'.

Betty was first of receive a reading from Crisp. Caitlyn sat near the chair but not close enough to distract Betty or Crisp. He was delicate and gentle in parts where Betty was emotional. She knew Betty would share everything with her after she had her own reading. Her reading lasted almost an hour.

During this time Caitlyn meditated. She had trained herself to hum a tune that created a vibration that went through her body. Caitlyn closed her eyes. This vibration turned into a soft drumming sound. A low tone that went through her. Her spine would align and the body would relax. When she reached a level of comfort and relaxation, her mind would clear and her inner vision would take over. Just like being in a theater, the curtains of her mind would open and a stage would appear. The vision or scene of being in a meadow would form. In her mind were flowers of all the colors and were big and bright. Trees in the distance fluttered their leaves at her. She could never tell where the wind came from. The sun was warm and bright. She looked out from being within and was there, in the meadow. Her vision was as if she was in her body, walking in the fields. When her head moved, the vision she held would change. Caitlyn reached this point in her mind as a place where she felt safe. She did not feel alone here. Unconditional love filled her heart. She could sense the fragrance of the flowers. She could feel the grass between her toes. The sunlight warmed every inch of her. She continued until Betty came to get her for her reading. Betty waited patiently until Caitlyn had finished. Betty talked all the way home about her reading with Crisp, while Caitlyn didn't have a change to share hers.

The day after the graduation, the parties came and went until early afternoon. Promises kept, Caitlyn loaded her things and was off as the sun reached its peak. She knows her way around having had many vacations when younger and more than one trip with kids from school. Field trips ended after days of world traveling. It seemed there were no limits to where they went. Caitlyn just wanted to be alone, to reflect on her dreams, to find answers. The direction she chooses was towards the mountains of the west. Something drew her towards the tall statues of peaks. Shadows created solitude in the darkness. Her vehicle pulled up to a path at the bottom of a ravine. Caitlyn knew there were cabins at different levels of her climb ahead of her. She had traveled until the sun was lower in the sky. She calculated about 2 hours of light before darkness would overtake her and she would need to find shelter.

Caitlyn had packed only what truly held something for her. Her backpack had her essentials and a large handbag of food from the kitchen ensured she would not be hungry. Caitlyn knew how to survive in the wild. Her many different classes had taught that. Part of the personal growth classes. She donned a light jacket, strapped on her backpack, picked up what remained and sent the vehicle back home. Now alone, she looked up the path again. Wondering what wonders she may find. Twenty minutes into the hike up the hill, the first clearing brought with it a small cabin.

Glancing at the sun, Caitlyn felt she could easily make it to the next level before darkness returned. It was as if each step forward enabled an awareness she had not known she had. She could see the plants and flowers along the path. They all seemed to have a glow about them. Trees were set back with an occasional branch reaching to the path. As she touched a branch she could feel the spark of life that it contained. Her mind gathered thoughts of seasons passing. Each branch she touched expressed a different view of the seasons. She began to feel the winds pick up as they gusted up the trail.

Dark clouds had formed and raced towards the peaks. Caitlyn picked up the pace. In no time she was feeling a light rain. At this height, she felt as if touching the clouds. The mist forming made it difficult to see the trail. More than once she found herself off the path. This time she could not find the path. The clouds obscured the sun and she could not tell direction. She could only follow the slope upwards. It stuck her as odd that she had not seen a bird nor animal on this path.

Harder the wind blew, more rain came. Her clothing began to absorb the rain. Her feet became heavy as the ground turned to mud. The path she had chosen became slick. She slipped to her knees. Her hands stopped her fall. 'Dang, I've got to be more careful' she said out loud. 'Soon you will know' she heard. It sounded like a voice right in front of her. She looked into the mist and could make out a second cabin. Somehow her senses had led her to the cabin. She rose from her knees and almost ran to the door. A simple turn of the door handle and she was inside. She closed the door behind her and took a deep breath of air. In the dim light she found an oil lamp and matches. Shedding her backpack and soaked jacket she felt a chill go through her. With the light of the lamp she took a look at her surroundings. Not a large cabin, but will be cozy and warm. She found the beginnings for a fire near the old stove. She had seen many pictures and movies with this entire cabin depicted.

Before long a fire crackled in the stove. She found another lamp and placed it across the room. The light from the two lanterns shared shadows along the walls. The shadows seemed to have a life of their own. Caitlyn knew of the fire, but shadows were new. They seemed to have an independence all their own. Feeling the warmth in the room spread from the fire, she shed her clothing and hung them to dry near the flames. Peeking in her backpack she found a dry shirt. She slipped it on and looked into the hand bag. She retrieved two power protein bars and sat in the middle of the room. Caitlyn nibbled on the bars and enjoyed their flavor. Pulling her knees up to her chest, hands on her knees, she rested. 'What a full and marvelous day' she said to herself. She reached forward, opened the door to the stove and placed a larger log into the flames. Sparkles of fire took off around the room. Zooming around then disappearing. 'Like a spark of life that had never existed' she thought. She closed the door to the stove and sat back.

Caitlyn's finally had a moment to think about her reading with Crisp. It seemed odd that he got so excited when he 'connected' to her Soul. 'You have a gorgeous aura of energy around you. Not any one color, more like a translucent, flowing rainbow. Each touch of his mind sends a different emotion to me. 'Do you have a feeling of being alone?' he asked. 'Like being from someplace else and that you don't belong here?' he continued. Caitlyn was about to answer when Crisp said, 'That's okay, please don't answer those questions. I feel that may be too personal. Let's move on. Crisp shuffled a tall deck of cards. She had seen Tarot cards before but these were different. Some cards had animals, some weird shapes and symbols and others still had pictures of the stars, of the universe.

Crisp explained. 'I have used these decks for many years. Each deck holds different energy. It's said in my family that the animal deck belonged to my great, great, great Grand Mother. Stories of her speak of her as an animal communicator, one that listens to animals. She was a Shaman as well. A healer. While placing the cards together one day, they leaped out of my hands onto the floor. I picked them up, all mixed together. I shuffled them and rolled the cards out for my daily reading and was astounded by the information that came through. The combination of cards told a better story. They come out in order of someone's life. I started using them in the services I performed and every time they proved to be of truth. I started asking the cards for future events and they have also proved to be truth. They can go far into the future of this lifetime. They can show what will happen today and tomorrow'.

Caitlyn thought for a moment, 'Do the cards allow selection of time when you want to know something specific?' 'Well, no, but they do come in order. They will pick out your life's events, past and future in this lifetime. You will know the meaning of the cards. Now you shuffle them three times and hand them to me'. Caitlyn did so and handed Crisp the large deck. 'Now cut the cards and place half in my other hand'. Caitlyn complied. Crisp took the top half and flipped the stack up on the table, showing the first card of the cut deck.

Crisp sat back, eyes open and said, 'Caitlyn, you are of a special breed of people. This card is the traveler. Meaning that you are not satisfied where you are'. From the other half, Crisp rolled the top card and smiled. The card showed a sun rise. 'You are leaving soon, possibly tomorrow, on a journey'. Now Caitlyn sat back in awe. 'You are surprised?' Crisp offered. 'Yes' Caitlyn responded. 'I will continue and you can listen. If you have any questions, please ask at that time'.

The next few cards showed big white fluffy clouds, a large hawk, and a cloud covered moon. 'The white clouds indicate the feeling of being aloft. Some call it out-of-body. The bird, large by standards, shows flight. Birds also are messengers. This bird seems to know you. Somewhere, wherever it is, is holding your heart. With the white cloud card, he appears to be a ruler of other birds. When flying high, he sees things from a different perspective. He is also a traveler. The covered moon means that you have to keep a watchful eye. Be aware of the events around you. 'Caitlyn, cut the cards in this stack' Caitlyn did as asked. The next card up showed a universe filled with galaxies. 'One day the traveler will appear to you and you both will go to far places. I see different worlds'. Caitlyn mused to herself. Her society had not developed interplanetary flight.

Caitlyn just listened, pondering Crisp's words. Doubt arose a little in her mind. Was this really true? Was she going to meet a traveler? Crisp broke into her thoughts, 'It will rain tomorrow, but not here. Where you are going, be cautious'. Crisp continued to talk about her family, their accident, the ambitions she had not shared with anyone. Her grades in school. The color of her aunts car. Soon, her hour was up.

Crisp picked up all of the cards and shuffled them. 'One final cut of the cards, please' Crisp requested. Caitlyn reached forward and held the full deck. She paused for a short moment, reflecting. What Crisp had said about her was true. What Crisp said about the future would need some thought and awareness of what she was looking for, or who she was looking for. Crisp rolled out three cards onto the table. He looked at her, focused on her eyes.

'Patience', the first card displayed. A small girl sparkly dressed, sitting on a large red stone coming up from the ground. She appeared to be scanning the horizon, waiting. A bright rainbow could be seen down one edge of the card representing the energy of the body. The second, a strange card representing the 'Elements' of the earth. Easy to pick out, the elements - earth, fire, water, air at the corners of the card. The rest of the card was jumbled, mixed at the edges and formed a spiral that seemed to sink into its middle. The third card, 'Awaken', showed a crystalline building or city, filled with bright lights on a black background. 'The Crystal City,' Crisp had added.

Caitlyn looked into the flames of the fire in the stove. She saw their dance. Each flame trying to out do the one next to it. 'Always competing, never winning'. As she looked at the flames her eyes seemed to go deeper in the flames. More flames appeared as if she was looking through the front line of flames. The colors seemed to change in her mind. Not keeping hold of the natural red color, but blues and greens as well. A small white light appeared in the flame. As she starred at the light she heard a voice calling to her. 'Jasper, Jasper, Jasper, soon you will know'.

Caitlyn closed her eyes and shook her head. When she reopened her eyes, the white light was gone. The colors remained. 'The colors must be from oils in the wood', she thought. She stood and pulled a night bag out of her pack. Pressing a small button to the side, it inflated into a nice firm mattress to keep her off the floor. A folded blanket was next.

Caitlyn then turned down the lamps until just a glimmer existed. Shadows began to grow. She body shook off the crazy thoughts of spirits in the night. She lay out on the mattress and pulled the blanket over her. She curled up so she could watch the flames in the stove. Her mind tried to sort the flames. They would not move, of course, but in her mind she could see different features in each flame. One particular flame seemed taller that the rest. It slowly grew until it was twice the size of the others. Curious, Caitlyn thought. Then she heard the voice again. 'Soon you will know'. The voice in her head caused her to sit up. 'Okay, where are you?' she said softly. Again she heard the voice, repeating the same phrase. 'Soon you will know'. Then silence.

The noise of the crackling fire diminished to nothing. The wind blew itself out and provided a stillness Caitlyn had never sensed. It felt as if her ears were plugged. Try as she did, she could not hear a noise. Caitlyn closed her eyes. In her mind the most wonderful panoramic view appeared. The view seemed to be a valley, similar to the valley below her. Trees and painted flowers abound. The sky held up huge puffy clouds. The sun, not too bright was behind her.

A form appeared slowly from the left, far in the distance. It did not seem to have a physical shape. As the form neared, she could make out a shimmering and glow about it. Closer the form came as at it did, it took shape. The form turned a golden brown color, easily 12 feet tall. She could make out wings and claws that carried the form on the ground. 'A bird' she exclaimed in her mind. Still sitting in silence, bird completed its formation into a solid shape. As it neared Caitlyn, the bird spoke to her 'Hello sister from another world'. 'Hello' Caitlyn responded. Caitlyn stood to greet her guest with some apprehension. 'You know who I am', the bird told her. 'Familiar but not too sure of your name', she replied, though she knew it was on the tip of her tongue. 'When last we were together, we were on a dying planet in a small galaxy not too distant from here. We had met only days before we departed that world. I searched for and found members of my kind. I have ruled many nations over many lifetimes. I have found a path that allows a continuance of those lifetimes'.

'Physical existence changes with each new surrounding lifetime, but the memories can be carried forward. You cannot return to the past and remember as memories cannot be changed once you choose this path. Lifetimes in the future are not cast in stone. They wait to be assembled, to be experienced. You sought your brother, the small boy from your family'.

"COMO" Caitlyn shouted and ran up to him. He lowered his massive head and she gave him a big hug around his neck. 'Como, I remember!' again shouting. 'You have crossed many lifetimes to get to where you are now. I knew you are here because your heart told you that he would be here. At our first meeting your name was Jasper. 'Caitlyn' she responded softly. This lifetime does carry all possibilities, as they all do. The choices you have made to be here, now, where written for you eons ago. Yes, your brother is here, and not too far away. He though is a lost soul here. He does not know of your choices, only feels the void of something missing within him. I am sure that is the same for you'.

Caitlyn sighed. A brother, from another lifetime. 'But he is not my brother. I have no brother here'. Como soothingly provided, 'He is the lost love, one of your Soul-mates. He too has been alone. To be alone has caused him great frustration and hardship. He travels like you, seeking an answer. He has had no family to watch over him. He has had no opportunity to share his heart. He knows not of the path we have taken, to be moving into different lifetimes to seek our truth. He will need to be taught, which I'm sure you can do.

'Where is he now?' she asked. 'He will arrive in several days from now. He is walking and broken. He trudges through his life with no hope for the future. Alone. You must show him his path, where he will journey. Yours and his can be one in this lifetime, and will continue if he chooses. Though many lifetimes ahead will not hold you together, many more will. Though you have awakened, you need to be more inside of your Soul to greet the traveler and to be able to guide him'.

Caitlyn closed her eyes. Visions formed in rapid succession of a rainbow of colors. Small balls of colors zoomed in and out and around her body. Traveling very fast she had difficulty in following just one. The balls of light seemed to be slowing and settling in a line, vertically in front of her. They settled just above her skin. They seemed familiar to Caitlyn. 'What do they mean?' she asked herself. She felt the warmth that was not there. The brilliance of the lights changed ever brighter. Each having its own journey to complete. One by one starting at the bottom, the red light, slowly moved toward her. It seemed to be getting hotter until she wanted to back away from it. As it touched her, a form of a flower formed, hovered and then disappeared within her. She felt the energy of the flower spread through her lower abdomen muscles leaving a tingling feeling, then fading. She felt a huge feeling of family, but at the same time a terrible feeling of being alone. Not missing her family, just the strength that a family offers. The next ball, orange, grew in brilliance like the first. Watching closely, the orange light came closer to her just below her belly button, forming a flower. This ball of energy entered her more swiftly than the red ball of light. Caitlyn held an overwhelming feeling of moving forward in her life but felt stuck. That's why she was here, to find that path. Impatience formed and growled deep inside her. The feeling created a cramping feeling and would not release her. It held a grip on her as she bent over to try to ease the pain. The pain twisted and molded her muscles and insides in ways they had not been positioned before this moment. The other lights waited their turn. When the cramping finally stopped, or at least eased to a more comfortable pain, each light blossomed into a flower and entered her.

Overwhelming feelings came with each color. Yellow filled her space just below her sternum, offering her emotions. Loves and fears emerged within her. Every emotion from fright to compassion came to her at the highest possible level. Green filled her heart, tears of compassion filled her. Sadness and loss formed a crack in her heart. A broken heart. Caitlyn understood now her feelings. Blue filled her voice. Respectful to others. She wanted to sing at the top of her lungs. Violet shook like a wet dog shaking the remaining water drops off after a cool rain. It bounced off her forehead and kept trying to get into her head. Seeming like forever, the violet ball finally entered her head. Caitlyn's head began to hurt, like a head ache. She squeezed her eyes shut and asked Como what was happening. 'These gifts of intuition are a weight to bear. When you decide to accept them, they will be part of what guides you. Right now, you have some gifts and a part of others. Accept the ones that you use now, that you are familiar with and your head with stop hurting. The others will emerge with practice'.

Caitlyn's headache eased and slowly evaporated. Her eyes opened to the indigo ball of light. It moved to the top of her head and hovered there. It lowered softly and gently to touch her head. Where it touched her it become an anchor for the strength of the light, traveling down her spine and out her feet into the earth. Then, BANG, at faster than light speed, the violet light took off towards the center of the universe. Stardust rained down around her and clung to her. When the violet light was too far away to see, an explosion of light appeared. The universe filled with more stars than Caitlyn had ever seen. All these stars created daylight around them. Caitlyn began to weep. Her heart became filled with unconditional love. The love of her higher self, creator. The crack in her heart healed and her abdomen stopped hurting. She felt her heart with her mind. 'I feel the universe within me. The love and compassion for everyone, every creature'.

She held no judgments of her past, no judgments at her losses in this lifetime. She took a deep breath. She felt the essence of her Soul within her cry with her. She was not alone. She never had been alone. Always, her essence had been with her. It had guided her to this lifetime and offered the challenges she needed to choose to complete.

Caitlyn looked up at Como, tears still in her eyes. He comforted her, holding her in his large wings. They both sank to the floor of the cabin as Caitlyn fell into a deep sleep. Caitlyn's mind stopped thinking for the first time in years, she did not dream. Como held her until the morning light had risen high in the sky.

Como had seen Jasper, uh, 'Caitlyn' many times in many lifetimes. Though she was lost, she was safe. Learning lessons that would guide her. His lives also had served him. Growth with awareness he was not familiar with. He too found his blue crystal, but just one lifetime ago. He had allowed himself to be the leader, never a lower class entity. His Ego had driven him to make hard decisions of life and death. To rob brothers and sisters of their youth and wealth. Como had mastered all presented to him. In all, his awareness brought all his memories with him as he traveled forward in lifetimes. As he sat holding Caitlyn, his sorrow grew great. He too had felt alone, like Jasper. His own despair of not knowing his Soul grew deeper and drove him with a huge void within him. Now he felt the pain Jasper had once felt. Now he knew the next step he must take. A tear formed in Como's eye. It dripped down his beak into the hair of Caitlyn. He too wept for truth, to know his own essence, his own Soul. To fill his void with unconditional love. Como had tried to bring alignment to his own rainbow colored balls of light. Sometimes getting close to feeling some of the energies inside him. Most often he would watch them circle his body and disappear. 'Next time', Como said quietly to himself.

Caitlyn moved slightly to begin the process of waking. She curled up tighter under his wing. She blinked her eyes, focusing on where she was. With a start, she jumped up and looked at Como, shaking her body and asking herself if this had been real. 'Yes, this is all true' Como offered to her mind. She dropped to the floor, crossed her legs and held her face, just starring at Como. As Caitlyn's foggy brain cleared and getting organized with these new experiences, all she could muster for words was, 'Oh My!'

Como stood and headed for the door. 'I will return when you have prepared yourself', and he was gone. Caitlyn rose and tried to do the morning things one does. The cabin did not have all the comforts of her home and a quick trip outside to a fallen tree provided well needed relief. Walking back to the cabin Caitlyn looked at the flowers that had grown reaching for the sun. When she had arrived the night before, it had been dark, raining and cool. Now the sun had dried the path. She took a little walk around the grounds of the cabin. Cut wood was piled along one side of the cabin. Looking around the corner of the cabin her eyes are drawn upward, following the structure of the mountain peaks above her. White caps of snow reflected the sunlight into the cabin area, opening the shadows around her. Caitlyn began to see things with her eyes open, waking up inside, feeling safe, feeling everything take alignment in her life. No fear. She did not feel alone any longer. She vowed not to allow those feelings to enter her thoughts or heart again.

As promised Como returned after having his own breakfast/lunch. 'There are many varieties of wild life for feeding on this planet. Quite a selection. Caitlyn, I tell you this from my heart. I have realized my path is not in this lifetime with you. I am moving toward lifetimes to seek my own inner path. While being with you has helped me see for the first time, this life is not complete for me to awaken as you have. Your path has been assembled for you. You will reach part of your dreams here, but more lives will follow as you continue to grow. As the traveler approaches, guard your heart. What seems on the outside will feel different on the inside, now that you are awake. I leave you now. Your energies follow me in all lifetimes. When you need me I will be there, a promise'. Como lowered his head and Caitlyn gave him a big hug. 'Como, I will miss you until we meet again'. Como flapped his large wings and soared into the sky.

Caitlyn watched as he circled higher and higher, riding the up draft of air currents driven by the mountains. Caitlyn knew he was leaving this world. 'How will he do that?' she asked herself. When he neared the top of the peak, still in view, he disappeared. In a thought he was gone.

The late morning had turned into a lazy afternoon. Caitlyn made some mental notes of the day. Wondrous things had begun to unfold in front of her. A new feeling inside her grew larger with the anxiety of life. Her pain of being alone was gone but still a void contained her wanting. She felt that the lifetimes of her past were coming together. Her dreams began of Jasper. Her short life in a distant past and a different place. She relived the events of Jasper's lifetime. She began to realize other lifetimes. Several being a male, some strong and bold, others meek and humble. She was beginning to see a common thread. One that connected them all. In each lifetime, a stranger appeared either before or after the event she witnessed, but always there. And one other thing, lightning. Lightning seemed to carry energy that proved involved with her loved ones, or directly at her. Her family from far away. Her lives as different people. A man who died like her brother, Keenyon, but was her. Her deaths carried the energy of her essence outwards into the universe, yet casting her stardust into the lifetimes presented to her many times did not show her the answers. She searched. Again and again she had looked for her companion. Is this the moment to find him? Como had said a traveler was coming.

As Caitlyn rested on a chair in front of the cabin she pondered the question of the blue crystal. She had seen it repeatedly in her dreams, always hovering, sometimes pulsing within her heart. Knew where it belonged but not where it had gone. She watched as the sun slowly lowered itself over the hills to the west. She had eaten little all day and felt a small growl. She moved slowly into the cabin, started a fire in the stove, grabbed a protein bar and sat on the bed. She was tired. Watching Como blink out of this world was really weird. 'How'd he do that?' She repeated to herself over and over again. Pulling the blanket out of her bag she laid down on the mattress. She was asleep within moments. Dreams came. All of her dreams had shown lifetimes that she remembered. Except this dream is different.

She could not close her eyes. She tries to but there are no eyelids. Lights are floating all around her. Some brighter than others but all sharing a moment in front of her before moving on its journey. 'Interesting' she thought. She felt mobile but sensing 'down' she had no body. Her color appeared blue to her. She could look in any direction. Her essence did not have form here. She pushed her mind to move forward, towards the others. They moved out of her way as she glided further than she thought she should have gone. Loud applause could be heard in her mind. But was it in her mind? But where was her mind if she didn't have a body. She pushed off again in a different direction.

Again the lights moved out of her way. Coasting, she looked around trying to find her way. Trying to find out where she was. Again applause filled her mind. It felt to her that she was taking her first steps. The first steps in a new existence. A beginning. In her she felt a feeling that only existed here. One of being complete, a wholeness. Am I a whole Soul? 'I am my Soul' the revelation hit her. The other lights gathered around her, coming into contact with her field of blue light. Each light shared a piece of themselves. She felt her own light grow as it accepted their offerings. Each held pieces of each other. By touching her living Soul, they are sharing their existence with her, forming a connection, a bond that will last for eternity. It became a familiar pattern as the lights continued to touch her, a new Soul. She had no memories of yesterday.

All around her she felt the grace of existence. The elegant glow of her blue Soul filled every molecule of her essence. As she gazed around she saw the Souls going to places where other new Souls came into existence. She felt so complete. She watched, then joined in with the others as they took turns touching the new Soul. She also observed new Souls' that did not get the touch of the others. 'they have other purpose' she knew. They would become light-beings, or angels. Knowledge of her path was forming for her. She could choose her path.

Like billions of Souls before her, she saw existence as a physical form. Many different forms for beings. Some as light beings, others of different worlds. All have a theme of joy and of being complete. Her illuminated blue Soul seemed now to have a purpose. She gazed into the world forming in front of her. A new world. Other Souls had chosen this world to start a path of learning. What lessons could this existence provide her? Who she would become was her choice.

She wandered to different worlds and found a young man and woman touching, sharing with looks into each other's eyes. She noted the colors. The male has blue eyes like the sky while the female has dark green, hazel eyes with an amber inner star pattern. She would choose the females eyes. She looked into their possibilities as life partners - mates. They had a strong bond of companionship. Both hard working. This world has three moons she noticed that gave the world a glow of reflected light. Even when not on the side of the sun, the darkness was broken and still able to faintly see into the shadows.

They called themselves human and carried names given them from their elders. T'Jon and Jada. In the early morning light they bonded, integrated by the physical union that produced the possibilities she had seen. Yes, she wanted to exist here. She wanted to experience these possibilities. She knew she could go anywhere to choose her path but this one seemed above the rest. 'Is this how it is for Souls? 'Her first physical existence?'

A short period after the enjoyable union she had watched. Her Soul essence entered the small grouping of cells forming the physical being within the human female. She grew rapidly and it seemed only a thought and she experienced the birth of her physical being. She did not feel alone, but filled with compassion and a feeling of being wanted. New emotions filled her Soul.

The pain of exiting the female. Her first breath, the warm feeling of flesh against hers. The sounds of the female at birth. She felt complete, tightly wrapped in her new mothers arms. She opened her blue eyes with an amber star pattern, seeing this new world for the first time.

She was given a name. As she grew over her first few weeks, the sounds of her name formed a familiar tone. That is her given name. Jasper.

Caitlyn woke to the sun peeking into the window. She remembered the dream as she stretched her muscles. 'Jasper?' Yes, had been her name. She felt different. She could feel that the emotions that had bothered her in the past were gone. She looked at the sun, feeling its warmth fill her. The vision of her blue light essence of her Soul being touched by others gave her a feeling of family. Of belonging. Caitlyn readied herself for the day and exited the cabin. She had emptied her bag and headed across the flatlands to pick roots and berries for her breakfast. Water flowed out of a small crack in the upper slope of the hills behind the cabin. She washed the fruits and roots and sat by a large red stone mass coming up from the ground. 'Jasper' she thought looking at the stone, like the name in my dream. That seemed odd that she had chosen to sit on this stone for breakfast. 'No such things as coincidence. This is my path and just another possibility'. She spent the morning and early afternoon climbing the slopes, investigating small caves and repeatedly examining her dream.

As the sun lowered and she returned to the cabin, she noticed the dark clouds forming. These clouds were darker that she had ever seen. The sky became dark purple. She saw lightning in the clouds, not touching the ground. 'Heat lightning' she remembered from a science class. Beautiful to look at but it could be just as dangerous and deadly as ground lightning. As the clouds became heavier, the winds picked up. She headed indoors. Far off, the lightning started to jump to the ground. An unknown fear entered her mind. She grabbed her blanket and mattress and huddled in a corner of the cabin, clear of the door and windows.

The sun began its disappearing trick as the lightning came closer. The wind howled through the cracks in the cabin walls. The flashes of lightning made the window glow like a flash bulb with each strike. She wanted to leave this world. 'How did Como do that?' the question popped into her mind. Her fears became real as several of the trees around the cabin began being struck by the lightning. Caitlyn could hear the trees exploding and crashing to the ground. Her heart jumped each time the thunder rolled into her mind. Fear gained a hold of her. She began to shake.

Without a warning, the thunder and lightning hit at the same time. The cabin door burst opened as if by an unseen force. Standing in the doorway appeared to be a ghost, illuminated by the lightning from outside. When the flash of light disappeared, darkness took over and a silhouette could be made out to be a man. He stood with his arms up, holding the frame of the door. Leaning forward, he fell to the floor, pushed by the wind and now hard rain. Caitlyn jumped up and scampered to the man. He was laying face down on the hard floor. Getting wet from the rain, she grabbed the man's collar and pulled with all her might to get the man inside. Drenched, she quickly closed the door. She leaned against the door to be a pillar, as if to keep the door closed. Taking several breaths, Caitlyn moved forward and lit a lantern to light the room.

Holding the lantern close to the man, see examined his clothing. A hiker no doubt. No, he wore a leather hide jacket and pants with tall moccasins covering is feet and ankles. 'Buckskins' she thought. His hair black like the darkness inside the stove. His shoulders broad and strong. On closer look, he appears to be Native American. His leather bag that he carried sported intricate bead work. It held a design she recognized as a thunderbird riding high in the sky. A large hunter's knife strapped to one calf. It too had intricate carvings in its handle and elaborate bead work on the sheathe.

He began to stir and Caitlyn backed away from him. He muttered something Caitlyn did not understand. He lifted himself to a sitting position and looked around the room. Spying Caitlyn, he said 'Sorry to barge in on you like that, but I have been running in front of this storm all afternoon. I knew of this place from many years ago. I didn't know you were here'.

Caitlyn was surprised at his perfect English with a slight deep growling accent. He stood up shedding his jacket and shook some of the water from it as he turned and hung the jacket on the large wooden knob on the back of the door. Water dripped into the puddle of water he had brought in with him. A little apprehensive, Caitlyn introduced herself saying, 'My name is Caitlyn. I've only been here a few days and I too have taken shelter here'. With that she became a little nervous as she stoked the ambers into fire in the stove for more heat.

Darkness was fully upon them now. Caitlyn lit the other lantern and really got a good look at her visitor. He hadn't moved from where he stood. He saw that Caitlyn was a bit nervous. In his own language he spoke words Caitlyn did not understand. He repeated in English, 'I am called Owatoma by my people. I am the orator, Animal Talker. I have been on a journey to recapture my Spirit. To regain who I am and who I am to be'.

Caitlyn became more at ease as they talked and shared their stories. Owatoma asked if he could remove his wet pants and shirt. A little embarrassed, Caitlyn offered her blanket to provide him some cover. She turned her attention to the stove to put her back to him. She glanced back a peek and she got a good look at her cabin mate. 'Wow' and she turned back, remembering every muscle ripple in his body. Caitlyn placed a pail of water on the stove to warm for tea.

Owatoma smiled and hung his pants and shirt over a chair near the stove. His hair still wet, he looked like he had just got out of a shower with the blanket wrapped around him. In his bag he retrieved a dry pair of pants. Caitlyn throw him her towel. He dried off the best he could and put his pants on. Both of them, a little more comfortable, continued the stories of each other's families. They both sipped the tea as Owatoma offered her some bread and dried meat from his bag. Caitlyn stood and placed her mattress across the room. She offered the old bed frame to Owatoma, who was happy to not have to sleep on the cool, hard floor.

Caitlyn lay down, blanket pulled up tight, she formed a tight ball and looked to her roommate. She watched as Owatoma lowered the wick in the lanterns to reduce the light and lay on the creaky boards of the bed frame. 'Could this be the traveler that Como said would appear?' Caitlyn wondered. She closed her eyes and took a few deep breathes. Centering herself in her heart she asked the question again. This time she felt her heart fill with compassion though did not feel this was the traveler. The feelings seemed familiar to her. She knew her heart to speak her truth. She felt this could be the traveler she was waiting for. Knowing this, she went to sleep. Caitlyn had a big smile on her face as the fears of the day vanished.

Owatoma was gone when she awoke. His dried pants and shirt were missing. She took a moment to straighten up the cabin. She felt renewed. She stepped outside to see

Owatoma beside a small fire. He had water boiling in an old pot from the cabin. In the pot he had placed roots and wild beans. 'I am brewing our midday meal. It will take a few hours for it to soften roots. We won't eat them, but the flavor is exquisite'. Caitlyn laughed, considering the words coming from this native man. The speech didn't fit the man. Definitely not what she would consider normal for the image she was looking at.

Owatoma stood and spoke to her in a voice she thought she remembered. 'While you slept, you spoke of someone named Como. Something about him vanishing before your eyes'. Caitlyn explained that Como had been in a previous lifetime with her. He was a giant bird that looked like a golden eagle clearly over10 feet talk. He also had come to this lifetime only a few days ago and had announced you coming. 'The traveler he called you. I know you are on a journey, but does 'traveler' make any sense to you?' Owatoma smiled. He began in his native tongue. It sounded like a prayer. 'I am a 'quantum-dimension shifter', is what you would call me. I do not really change my shape. I have been given a gift to cross dimensions. Time means little to me'. At hearing this, Caitlyn recalled some studies of quantum mechanics and string theory. She had thought them boring at the time.

Now Owatoma had her complete attention. 'By shifting my energy to a very high vibration I appear to those here then I disappear. It's like I move out of phase with where I am.

When in another dimension I become almost solid again, each has a possibly for events and people to cross your path. I was told many years ago by the ancient shaman in my tribe that I was to teach a woman the basics of shifting. I believe you are the one, especially after listening to your dreams. Each possibility is similar, and I have seen you before, but not recognized you in this lifetime.

Caitlyn recounted her dream just two nights before when she had become the essence of her Soul. Owatoma commented, 'By doing so you have raised your own vibration to a very high level. I know you have experienced this before, both now and several lifetimes ago. Each of us has special gifts for each of these journey's we partake. While I have not experienced your gift, I will teach you to shift. To maybe help find your friend'.

He asked Caitlyn to sit facing the fire. She felt its warmth as she knelt and then slid her legs out from under and sat down on the edge of the blanket. She crossed her legs in a yoga type position, spine straight and looked into the fire. Her hands rested in her lap. As in the cabin, she saw the flickering of the flames testing each other. As she looked, her head became lighter, then her body seemed to have no feeling. Owatoma spoke softly in his tongue. 'Fears will not exist here. You will have full memory of your visions and travel. I will be with you. Take a long deep breath and hold, hold, hold, and release. Push your breath out. Relax'.

Owatoma held a small silver box in the palm of his hand, almost like a small remote control. Using his finger tip he gently pressed several symbols. Ω ‡ ◊ Δ ∑ £ ∞ Each symbol having its own meaning. She watched him press the sequence and was astonished by the view of the fire, of the cabin, of the hills around them. They were not shimmering, but more like of a wave of light passed over them. They became translucent, flowing as they watched. The fire disappeared. The sun remained in its position but their surroundings changed, they became many seasons, summer, fall, winter. Owatoma asked for her hand. When they touched they were placed into a reality that Caitlyn did not recognize. Fully visible to them, the country side had changed into a sprawling suburban village.

Owatoma stood and assisted Caitlyn to her feet. 'This is a parallel dimension. Similar to ours but another possibility. We have not traveled in time, we only have drifted into the next dimension. There are many dimensions, choices if you'd like'. 'The box', still in Owatoma's hand, he continued, 'is a portal generator, opening a window into the next dimension. It allows us to 'shift' our presence. Many possibilities can be accessed from these life-times. It is similar to a spider's web. Each lifetime, connected to many. By guiding our thoughts, we are able to move and see these realities. You can interact and stay here if you are pleased, though you will no longer exist in the other dimension. Your energy will take solid form here. I will add this for you as well. Not all possibilities are pleasant. Many have had their worlds destroyed by fear, greed and control. This dimension is similar to our own, though the populace is less developed. More of a middle culture, if you will. Not as advanced as yours'.

Caitlyn was in awe of what she was seeing. This dimension gave her comfort. She liked the colors and 'pace' that this world was operating at. Everything seemed just right. Owatoma pointed up to the sky. 'There are two moons here. They create an imbalance to the rotation and it causes the world to wobble. Seasons are very short. They have almost two seasons to our one. Plants do not grow as they would in our place. Small but full of nutrition. I'm sure you can imagine other places like this. I will show you now this dimension with a time shift. The effect is similar though we will jump ahead several hundred summers'. They hadn't moved from the original camp fire. Owatoma raised the silver box and again pressed the symbols with his finger tip. Œ ø ð § π The sun changed color as they zipped into the future. The warmth did not seem complete. The world had suffered from the uneven rotation. Great earthquakes had caused the planet to have many rifts. The suburban village no longer exists, flatted and over grown by vegetation. The sky had also changed color to an amber from the dust in the air. The earth rumbled under their feet. 'It is not safe here, as we would not be safe in our own time. Hold my hand' Owatoma palmed the silver box and reversed the order he had pressed earlier to create the shift in time.

Instantly they appeared to be back at the entry point of this dimension. The village reappeared as it was. 'We can stay here for as long as you'd like. We can also jump into the other dimensions that exit from here'. Caitlyn looked around. This village did not seem the same as there last visit. Slight differences in the roof structures, the colors not as comforting. 'Has something changed by our visit here? Caitlyn asked. Owatoma also took stock in the area around them. The vegetation had changed. 'It appears that there may have been visitors that have traveled into the past from this point in time. My elders had said that if we change the past the future will be changed as well. Come, we must go now'. Owatoma thumbed the silver box and instantly they appeared back at the cabin and fire. The fire was still burning. 'We have not missed any time in this dimension. All as it was when we left. No time has passed here'. Caitlyn looked around and confirmed that they were indeed back to their starting point.

Caitlyn spoke first. 'I am truly amazed at the ability of your silver box to shift dimensions. I am a little confused by the need to leave the time of the future when we did'. Owatoma explained, 'That time showed the end of that world. We were not in danger but the image of that time was going to cease to exist. We are permitted to go to the past only as observers. We are only an essence of ourselves in the past. Interaction with the physical beings and environment can change the future. Think of it as being in a past life. Actions that have occurred in the past can be brought forward into this lifetime. It is similar to the cell memory that our scientists have discovered many years ago. We can travel to the past only as an observer. That is what the silver box does. When in the future, we are in a more physical form, still only as an observer. We cannot place a change there that will stay. When we return to our time, the interaction returns to its former self. We have observed other travelers from other dimensions. They are seen as flying ships in different forms. There are many different life forms that visit this world and its dimensions. They appear and then seem to disappear. They do not have the time travel capabilities but can travel where they want in any dimensional shift'. It is how they can travel the great distances of the universe. 'Como?' Caitlyn thought.

Owatoma continued, 'In my tribe many of us have learned to jump dimensions without the need for the silver box. I have not and need the aid of the silver box. It is from another parallel dimension. You have the control and power within you to focus yourself into a place where you will be able to seek a dimension that you would like to visit. 'And you will teach me?' Caitlyn asked. 'Yes, tomorrow. We will rest for the remainder of the day'. Caitlyn felt she had a need to be alone, to reflect on the information her mind had just acquired. She stepped away from Owatoma and walked towards the path. 'I will return shortly, I need to think'. All that she knew did not cover this topic of dimensional shifts.

As Caitlyn walked the path, her mind wondered. She did not look to see what was in front of her, but intuitively her feet kept her safe. Dimensional shifts. Time travel. How very different from what she knew. The possibilities intrigued her. She had a sudden thought of Como. Is this what he had done when he disappeared in the sky? Jumped to another dimension? Caitlyn found a tree with a large base and sat next to it. She closed her eyes. She felt exhausted. She sat for some time. She listened. Just to be quiet was great. She sensed vibrations in the earth and the tree that held her back straight. The vibrations were not strong. The vibration turned into a hum. The hum rose from her feet, up her legs and slowly up her back. It was aligning her spine. When she felt her neck relax she knew the humming vibration was going to encompass her. Still with eyes closed, she felt the very core of her body release all tension. She felt herself moving backwards, into the tree.

The tree welcomed her. She could feel the grace in the life energy of the tree. Caitlyn's own energy stood and the tree accepted her. She could see out from the inside of the tree. 'Welcome' she heard in her mind. Startled, Caitlyn turned slightly as if to see behind her. 'Welcome' she heard again. 'Hello' was her response. 'Who are you?' 'I am the Spirit of this Tree. We all have many names though you would not understand most of them. We hold the wisdom of the others before you. Your kind each has many trees that honor you. We trees can span many of your lifetimes. We all have contact to the earth below. We all have a vibration or hum that identifies us in a certain way, yet, we are all individual, all unique in who we are. The Spirit we hold is from the beginning. Before a single seed fell to the ground to grow we where an essence, a Spirit with our creator. We have spread through the universe to hold the knowledge and wisdom you ask for. Many like you have found us. Most do not see us. Those that do, return to live a different path. You call it nature. Some are shunned for their choice. Some lead others. We all seek the same truths. Will you choose to become part of us? We do not know. Our goal is only to be here to answer your questions, to help guide you'. Caitlyn took some time before responding to the tree. She felt safe and comfortable.

All those questions like 'What is my purpose in life? Who is my Soul mate? What career path should I take?' flooded her mind. 'Relax', the tree said, 'breathe'. 'The purpose in life is to find inner happiness. Nothing more, nothing less. The path presented to you offers a choice of a path to find true joy. The obstacles put in your path are lessons to learn from to give you the tools to reach your goals. The people in your past have the same purpose. We all find solace in finding like Souls, with like hearts with a like inner light. We seek beings that give us the feeling of grace with gratitude. It starts as a friendship. An understanding of each other's needs and a bonding occurs. Souls touch. Happiness is shared, along with your failures. We create in our minds the negative emotions, stirring the ego out of its slumber. The ego grows to contain us. It allows your mind to create feelings, fearful emotions, and doubts about who you are. It hides your path with quilt. It shadows your thoughts with loneliness. You are but children when it comes to seeing with your heart. What frightens you is what you create in your mind and heart. You cannot be hurt by what you create yet it feeds the ego with fears. Misguidance is the result of false footings. Loose roots, if you will. If your faith and path are not clear, you will not know what direction to follow. How do you feel about your life in this moment?'

Caitlyn was in awe. The tree had read her heart to its core. A vibration of the tree filled her and with it every cell released its torture being held by the ego. Caitlyn searched for the proper words to respond to the tree. 'I feel that the creation of nothingness in me is filled. You have shown me myself. You have given me courage to see the lessons that you teach and the lessons that I receive. You have shown me a smile that has been hidden in me and given my fate laid out before me. The history of my life, like the lines in my hands show a past and a future. You have given me the wishes and dreams that I had not the bravery to find. The future I create is for my Soul. To complete the commitment to find my Soul mate. The twin of my Soul, who has trust in me and that I will have trust, and share that trust with others as the trust I have in myself. I offer you honor of your wisdom, of your guidance'.

Caitlyn leaned forward and her essence merged with her physical self. Her eyes opened wide and she took a deep breath. She stood up and turned to face the tree. With little effort she reached around the tree and gave it a huge hug, 'Thank you again for your wisdom'. Caitlyn returned to the path and found her way back to the camp. She found Owatoma knelt by the fire, still stirring the pot contents.

Owatoma spoke first, 'I see that your glow has changed. It seems you have found part of you that has been lost for some time. A child of you. Please sit and share your story'. Caitlyn drew pictures in her mind of her visit with the Wisdom tree. 'I believe the tree has offered me a choice in my path. Though it wasn't mentioned, the tree knew my Heart'. Owatoma served the stew and they ate in silence.

When dinner was finished, Owatoma asked, 'Do you feel up to learning the tool of dimension shifting?' 'Oh yes', Caitlyn replied without a second thought. 'Very well, lay down here on this blanket. Get comfortable. Close your eyes. I will guide you to the edge of this dimension. I will not follow. Your thoughts will guide you to the dimension you seek. You can return here with a thought of where you are right now at anytime. Remember, you are an observer and cannot interact inside a dimension you do not belong'.

'Breathe deeply and relax. Each breath makes you deeper relaxed. Deeper and deeper relaxed. Feel the ground below you. Feel the vibration pulsing of the land around you. Feel the vibration center below you. You can feel the waves of energy being released into you. Each wave of energy creates a vibration equal to the incoming pulses. You can feel your entire body engulfed by the vibration. You can see to the cellular level. Watching the pulses enter each cell, you can see the infinitely small particles of the cell being stimulated. Further still you are seeing smaller, into each cell. The chromosomes and other components of each cell. A wave of vibration causes the cells interior to oscillate. Smaller still, you can see the molecules and then the atoms of the cells. You focus on one atom. It looks like a small solar system, electrons orbiting a nucleus. As you get near they become larger. The space between them increases. Empty space between them. You can enter the space and feel the forces holding the rotation of the electrons in place. Unknown forces. As you enter the well of energy, you are transported to a different place. You see the two portals floating around you. You can choose which portal you will take. The nearest is available to you. A parallel dimension. You can feel a shift in presence around you. The atom's energy appears the same, but for a slight difference. You focus on the feeling of this difference and instantly appear as yourself, but in a different place. Caitlyn looked around to see the sight of her visit with Owatoma. She stood alone. Taking a breath to relax, she returned to the size of herself within the atom. Again two portals appeared. She chose again. This time she felt a tingle of guilt. She opened her eyes to see a city with tall spires in the far distance. Very similar to her own dimension. Valleys filled with flowers surrounded her. People walked the paths in the valley nearest her. She could feel the emotion of a young couple walking hand in hand. They paused and looked at each other's eyes. She could feel the intention behind the gaze. Suddenly, the man disappeared. Startled, Caitlyn felt an overwhelming feeling of abandonment and of being alone. Her heart swelled in sadness. 'No' came a gasp. 'Why do I continue to feel this way?' She did not want to stay here any longer. She opened her mind to returning to her place at the cabin. With a small jolt, she opened her eyes and knew she had returned.

Owatoma sat nearby. He had watched during Caitlyn's journey. She eyes were swollen with tears. Caitlyn broke into a sobbing. She could not catch her breath. Owatoma reached to her and held her tightly in his strong arms. A feeling of protection came over Caitlyn. Owatoma's strong but gentle touch calmed her. Her breathing eased and she regained control of her tears. Owatoma looked into her eyes. He could see the depth of life Caitlyn carried. He moved his lips closer to hers and they touched. Both of them melted into one. They held the embrace, enjoying the moment. Caitlyn broke the kiss first. She looked into his dark eyes. She felt more complete than she ever had. His touch lingered where she stood. Breaking the embrace, she walked to the other side of the camp fire and said a little embarrassed, 'I need to clear my head for a moment'.

She walked towards the cabin, entered and closed the door. The coolness of the room entered her being. She lay down on her mattress and closed her eyes. Flashes of the recent past events entered her mind. The thoughts always ended up with her in Owatoma's arms. Sleep came over her. An hour later she awoke, refreshed but still a bit frazzled.

Darkness was nearing when she opened the cabin door and looked out she was gripped in sadness. The fire was out and Owatoma was nowhere to be seen. She called for him, but no answer came. "Was Owatoma the traveler?' she thought. 'I am alone. How do you know what lifetime you are experiencing', Caitlyn wondered. 'Do the lifetimes of the past and the future all come together where you are in that moment, and that the thought of them creates them?' So may questions. So many things she did not understand.

In her mind she heard, 'Soon you will know'.

Evening clouds and an oncoming storm drifted up the valley. The wind howled its' ominous story. Lightning crackled and the thunder spoke loudly.

Caitlyn gathered her blanket and closed the door of the cabin. The stove still held embers from the fire it held just this morning. As Caitlyn placed kindling on the embers, the kindling leaped to life. A small fire produced the added effect of a radiance of warmth. Though it was not cold, the difference in temperature from the front side to her back side made her feel a little jumpy. A shiver that started in her neck raced down to her tailbone, causing her back to arch. She stood up too fast, a little dizzy from the events of the day and the toll taken.

The kindling that she had been handling missed the entry into the stove and parts hung over the doors edge. Caitlyn felt a little light headed and looked for her blanket. Now lying on the bed frame, the firmness of it made her stretch. Reaching for the blanket she then wrapped it tightly around her. Caitlyn lay on the frame and it felt good on her back as her muscles began to relax. 'What is all this about?' she asked herself. The Traveler had not appeared, though she thought Owatoma may have been him. Como said the traveler was her brother. Caitlyn closed her eyes again, to relax and to clear her mind.

In the corner of the room, the stove started to sing as the smaller flames grew, eating away at the wood in its belly. The small kindling that hung out the still open door burned slowly, creeping out of the confinement that the stove held. Small strings of the kindling, still burning, dropped to the floor as the stove doorway let them go. The floor was covered with a fine dust from the aging of the friendly cabin. Small sparks from the kindling seemed to become small steps. Each step getting bolder. Each step leaving a burning footprint. The small footprints grew together looking like a snake as they ignited every particle of dust and other toothpick sized pieces of wood. Soon the small flames turned to larger flames and the floor itself burned. The combined fires drew the flames out of the stove. Smoke started to fill the room.

Caitlyn had fallen asleep, unaware of the fires and smoke, and did not notice the lack of oxygen getting into her lungs. And finally, painlessly, her mind closed within itself. Caitlyn died, physically. Her essence escaped the physical vessel she was using for this life experience by leaving her body. Smoke and flames consumed the small cabin.

Her essence floated above her body. She rose through the roof of the cabin just as it exploded from a huge bolt of lightning, forcing the walls and ceiling to collapse. The fire was instantly put out by the blast. The rubble and dust settled over her body. The flash triggered a memory, something from her past.

The burnt down cabin and her body were found three days later by a 'traveler'. He had been shown to come to this area by a psychic named Crisp. The psychic had told him that he was to find a lost soul here. A sister from a past life.

The essence of Caitlyn/Thomas/Jasper and other lifetimes hung in the sky, searching for a direction, a path to follow. In this form, great joy filled her. She felt complete. Not a physical being any longer, human contact was not a requirement to become fulfilled. She drifted aloft rethinking the recent lifetime, rethinking the opportunities it had given her. Rethinking the message of the trees, Owatoma and the humbling experience of dying.

Her lifetimes appeared before her.

Caitlyn has experienced the choices she has made.

Dimensional travel; body vibration changes

Time travel

Psychic reading abilities

Visualization and Imagery

Remembering - Returning to be the essence of her Soul

'Is this all I do? Floating around, rethinking past lives and their lessons? Are the lesson's the same for all essences of life?' A look inside herself found Jasper, her first human experience. She had been so young, so adventurous. Jasper's short life zipped past her. The light-being recognized at the end of Jasper's existence seemed to materialize in front of her.

'You have been gone for a large portion of your total existence, yet you have the questions of a new soul. Your feelings of being alone have been your ego fodder for many lifetimes. Many lifetimes send you on a personal journey to become complete. While you have come close, and have had many times to having a loving companion, the effect of being alone still lingers. It fills your heart with fear. This fear contains emotions, feelings, and an underlying craving to fill the void created by ego. Where does your mind and heart wander? The feeling of being alone portrays your self-worth, and how you feel about yourself. Like kids playing, when you do not feel great about who you are, the 'I'm not as good as they are' takes over. 'I'm not worthy. Don't pick me!' You'd shout, 'pick him or her' and do not look at yourself. It is judgment of yourself when comparing yourself to others.

These are lifetimes created by you, are intertwined with many other of your soul's lifetimes. You see some Soul lifetimes daily, others only on occasion. Each has their own journey to travel. You are part of their journey as they are part of yours. Each lifetime carries the elements to become complete. You do not have to relive a past life to heal yourself today. Worry is just a tool for the ego. Fear of being alone is just a small part of your lesson. What are the gifts that are attached to this feeling? Independence - self-confidence? You have to do the work. Clarity, self love and common goals, and visions of a future, not of a past. Your eyes point to the direction of the stars. They contain your path and all who will meet you. The Others. The ones that see your depth, your perseverance, your attitude towards others and yourself are qualities that only a few achieve excellence. Take heart in who you are and will become. The echoes of the trees around you send glorified greetings. They too know your true potential, they know your path'.

'When you listen with your heart, and to the spirits around you, the ear falls silent to the ego inside. Be open to the courage that wants to come out and play. To not hide from the commitments that are continually changing in polarity. Look to the imagined future, and what you want to create. When quiet inside, your heart seems to listen best and know you are not alone'.

With that, the light-being pointed to the stars. The lights of the lifetimes she had experienced seem to fade. All faded but one, glimmering with excitement. The new opportunity grew brighter. Her inner blue crystal essence glowed brighter than ever before. It appeared as a bright star on a very black sky at night. Boldly the essence of all of her slipped forward into this lifetime. The trees echo can still be heard. The animals chattered with excitement at the arrival of a new Soul eager for the lessons of this new lifetime.

'Now you know'

This lifetime seems different from the rest, boldly selecting a family unit with an older sister. The Soul also sees two other Soul essences, which appear to be waiting. They have selected to wait for the next two births. They will be boys too. 'Great, someone to grow up with', the Soul essence comments. A new lifetime, ready to guide me on a twisted life path. This might be the life that the 'Traveler' reunites with this original Soul.

Each lesson comes with the knowledge of advancing the Soul to a higher level of completion of its charter. Each lifetime carries the challenges for the Soul to witness and experience, yet the memories of other life-times echo across the universe.

A boy of average size and stature. Maybe a little chucky for his age. Mama always gave him the extra scoop to reduce leftovers. Mama always knew where he was, hiding or not, he always had to review his day and say where he had been. 'Stay away from the train tracks' she'd say. But she knew if he crossed them as a shortcut to get home. A lesson here to learn. School did not come easy. He tried hard to get his homework done. He never asked for help. He was different from the others in the family. He knew at a young age that he would be different in the future as well, but in what way, he did not see. No college, money was tight.

Mom and Dad divorced and then his Dad he passed at age 42. A surprise to all. Some weird disease called leukemia. He passed quickly, four days later after testing. He had been a warrior in the Navy. A flyer and radioman. Fought with the best in the South Pacific. 'A hero in my heart', even though the problems at home created a different 'him'. His brothers also served and honor goes to them too.

After high school, a choice is offered for service. He too joined to serve. More world conflict and he thought he could escape it. But it was not to be. He had to make a choice. A soul's choice was to continue forward, regain the experiences awaiting him. 'Allow him to grow up', they'd say. And he did. He excelled at the challenges he faced. More schooling followed him, every corner had something new to learn. To this day, he learns things that interests him, that help keep the void inside away.

Marriage, children, mortgages and pets filled his life. A huge conflict was cooking and burning inside of him. Mom passed too at 53. Unknowingly he had been growing inside, nurturing the experiences this life-time had offered. When the phone rang, knowing who was calling at better than 85% of the time (before caller ID!). Déjà vu, telepathy, energy sensitivity. These little pieces of life offered a different view. He's tasted many religions and though never was settling for the choices offered. Always questioning theology as new information was presented to an alternative. 'What do I do', he'd cry. A little uncommon release of emotion for his middle years.

His choices had mostly been good. Achieving higher positions in companies that feed him. He still felt a void within him. A void he could not describe, only carry it every day until his choices changed. Instead of working with every else around him he chose to go within himself. Mystery and miracles surrounded him. He had heard of 'awareness' but wasn't sure he wanted anything to do with it. It seemed to create a conflict with his family and with his work. But he didn't care. He studied self-healing and followed a clearer path. His beliefs changed to search for the 'inner-self', finding the IAM was not out of his reach.

Miracles approached him and he accepted them willingly, seeing the outcome of the current choices and providing a new understanding of who he had become. Angels appeared when he asked for help. He learned of the tasks they do for him. He embraced others of the same path, seeking a companion to share his ideas and beliefs. More study. Psychology, Hypnosis, physiology, ThetaHealer, anatomy, medical intuition becomes real to him. Energy healer some called him. Shaman others call him. Life is pleasant when he went inside himself. He begins to integrate the gifts, to have instant access to his past and the gifts other lifetimes had offered. Outwardly, bitter at times, he continues the obligations to a physical life, still seeking the 'others' that can complete this lifetime, the inner lights that he shares are in his heart.

his Soul has experienced;
Guided Imagery
Channeling
Telepathy
Empathic Emotions
Clairsentience
Clairvoyance
Medical Intuitive
Prophetic knowing
Reiki
And more

This life time is not complete. He knows of more he wants to learn. To be the healer he himself has grown into. Daily life offers opportunities. A smile, a hug, and a few guided words all help to change lives, to offer more clarity and more choices.

The Essence of Jasper/Thomas/Caitlyn/Him, all have similar lifetime experiences, being given an opportunity to experience their gifts. Many more lifetimes are in their future, each holding an opportunity for the Soul to learn the lessons of its existence. It is not strange that the Soul's goals differ from our own. And it can take lifetimes to recognize your intuition. We all carry these tools. We just need to learn to listen.

I have been an 'intuitive' all of my life. I just wasn't 'aware' of the opportunities being presented until later in my life. Sure I've had those moments but never connected them together. I have chosen many different career paths, each provided what I felt driven to receive and needed for that time in my life. Each choice was made due to an unknown frustration deep within me. Places and people I worked with all played a role. By changing positions I grew in personality, job experience and people skills. Though they all have had a basic underlying theme in a technical environment, the vast challenges with variety always drove me and still does.

The Soul does not recognize time as we know it. For the soul, all past life times are right now, providing instant access to the information for any of the Soul's lifetimes. My own 'Soul's history' has been described to me as a spider web, though yours may vary. Each lifetime is connected to all others, each sharing memories and information about that lifetime. I've been called a 'healer' at times where the healing 'expert' of a past life actually steps up and becomes the 'resident healer' for that specific healing. Some people might call this 'channeling'. I have experienced the Shaman, Spiritual leaders, and medical experts and others from many fields. That passing of knowledge and energy is tremendous. I've only had to learn to listen. And I listen very, very well.

We have one analogy of past lives in this lifetime. I have witnessed my own evolution of who I am, just as you have. Just look at your own pictures from birth until now. I know there were times when material items were the most important things in my life. Keeping up with your neighbors was always the challenge in that moment.

I can remember at least five different 'me' in this lifetime. The late teen-early to twenties, the mid twenties and into the thirties. I remember the disco days and being dressed in a pink shirt. (I still wear pink occasionally!) Weight gains and losses. Job changes and more all have been different lifetimes for me. Goals change, our faces change, new meanings of old choices we've made become clear as new choices are presented to help create the next lifetime.

In my mid thirties something changed. Medical issues arouse from a hereditary condition. I felt I was being dumped on. Work, home, just about everything needed change. My life changed rapidly into a turmoil that I could not control and didn't know how. I asked the universe for help. Wow, does the universe ever listen! Holistic professionals, spiritual people and different practitioners began to make themselves known to me. I immediately decided this was a path that I wanted to be on. Over several years I was introduced to classes of different modalities. Training in these opened me up even more. My gifts re-awakened and now there is not a day that they aren't with me.

As time goes on, other opportunities present themselves. On an occasion to be with some light hearted friends, we had been discussing past lives. Being a CMHt, I have conducted more than a fair share of regression healings. Past lives turn out to be a common request. While past lives can and do play a role in pattern problems, it is important to understand what the issue in this life time. My philosophy has always been to heal the current issue in this lifetime. The journey to past lives is an exhilarating experience. Early on I had asked a client to return to a past life that reflects the same issue that they had just healed. On one such occasion, I also asked the client to return to their first experience. I assumed they would go to the first human occurrence of their issue. Wow! What a completely eye opening event.

I'll not describe the Souls' origin here but need you to know that all of my clients experience the same event or 'place', and descriptions vary only slightly. They all describe the 'Soul's Nursery', our point of creation. The time between lives. Where we return to be our essence.

This life-time is the important one. There is only one journey, only for you. Your Path and the choices you've made can lead you to new found gifts and hopefully . . . your Soul.

As we grow and experience this lifetime, our awareness and intuition awaken. The lifetimes of our past reveal the steps we earn to meet our 'Essence of the Soul'. Our 'Essence' lives, from its origin and between our lifetimes.

Ask yourself, 'Which lifetime am I living?' Each piece of the Soul's experience make you who you are today. Learn to see this lifetime from your Soul's perspective and claim your gifts. You can follow the Soul's journey to awareness.

See how the Soul in this lifetime, one that can offer new knowledge and new opportunities, yet carry with it the memories of its existence. Gain honour for the lifetimes it has lived and share in its experience of the lifetimes of loss.

This book presented to you gives a glimpse of our internal power demonstrated in these lifetimes. The Soul's existence is eternal and this story has no end. Maybe your lifetime belongs here.

Join *your* Soul. You will find your Soul and share in its experiences and marvel at the trials of living that we all share. ~ John E. Peterson 2011

Note: In this last lifetime, the Soul has not chosen a name. Though, if you know me, than you may have recognized part of my lifetime. I am not afraid of thunder, but lightning, well....

Share your story. This one I offer here can be yours too.

For my friends that travel with me in my heart, I honor your guidance, your sometimes wisdom and sometimes your choices. I believe all Soul's that we meet; we have met before, in this and other life-times. Greet the Soul beside you and acknowledge their journey. For it is not your place to judge their choices, but to ask them if you can travel with them. ~~ John

John E. Peterson can be reached at john@psy-guy.com.

www.ingramcontent.com/pod-product-compliance
Ingram Content Group UK Ltd.
Pitfield, Milton Keynes, MK11 3LW, UK
UKHW041933190726
13854UKWH00004B/1568

9 781105 056147